WRITING YOUR WAY

—

A Writing Workshop for Advanced Learners

—

MARTHA GRAVES CUMMINGS
RHONA B. GENZEL

Heinle & Heinle Publishers
A Division of Wadsworth, Inc.
Boston, Massachusetts 02116 U.S.A.

For George, Brette, Rob, and Aunt Charlotte
and
for George, Rose, Gene, Aimee, and Jenny

ACKNOWLEDGMENTS: We would like to extend thanks to our many colleagues who have shared stories of success and triumph as they helped students improve their written communication skills. Particular thanks go to Jo Burgoyne Cone who, with the keen observation of an experienced writing instructor and the spirit and enthusiasm of a good friend, read this manuscript offering suggestions and even contributing a piece of writing to exemplify the use of half sentence transitions. Thanks also go to Janene Oettel and Janet Heyneman who reviewed parts of the manuscript and offered suggestions. We also extend our appreciation to Judith Slade and Ed Cain who suggested experiments for the section on chemistry and writing lab reports. Special thanks go to those students who have granted us permission to use their material: Heidi Simmons, Manuel Rodriguez, Jonathan Cohen, Jeff Starr, Robert Costello, Dawn Medeiros, Nadeem Vakil, Timothy A. Robinson, Tim Coffey, Paul Piciocchi, Jeffrey Maynard, Miriam Schwab, Scott Mansfield, Tamera Slavik, Enrique Arce, Zulay Maldonado, John Kroetz, Timothy Perusse, John J. Grieco Jr., Nick Kim, Stacy Zaslow, Jennifer Janaitis, Samer Raad, Sasson Posner, Ronald Manginell, Mike Bendure, Blaise Miller, Peter E. Cimmet, John C. Carlson, Alan H. Flint Jr., Douglas M. Niven, Steven E. Ludwig, Amy L. Pocock, David Weiner.

Writing Your Way: A Writing Workshop for Advanced Learners

ISBN 0-8384-2953-X

Library of Congress Cataloging in Publication Data

Cummings, Martha Graves.
    Writing your way: a writing workshop for advanced learners /
Martha Graves Cummings, Rhona B. Genzel.
      p. cm.
    Includes index.

    1. English language—Rhetoric. 2. English language—Textbooks for foreign speakers. I. Genzel, Rhona B. II. Title.
PE1408.C77 1989   89-2871
808'.042—dc19   CIP

91 92 9 8 7 6 5 4 3

Contents

To the Teacher

Writing Your Way uses a workshop approach to show students that writing can be an interesting and exciting subject. For years, we, like so many teachers of English or Freshman Composition, have been faced with unwilling students who see no reason to be able to write well and who are intimidated by the subject.

We set out to prove to our students that writing is important now and in their future. We helped our students take an active role in thinking through their writing and in critiquing their work. The result of these efforts is the text *Writing Your Way*.

In *Writing Your Way*, students gain control over writing as they gain insight into the communication process. They come to realize the importance of writing as they work through a variety of practical writing assignments. These assignments include answering short answer questions and writing a business letter. Students also learn research techniques and the information required to develop a research paper. Through debate, they become involved and excited about research and have an opportunity to test their ideas before actually writing their research papers.

Writing Your Way is an advanced level writing text designed to be used in English composition classes at the college level or with advanced level English as a second language students. The text has been used successfully with both American and international students. It should be used in conjunction with a handbook of English.

The text has been designed to flow from a study of the concept of audience, to answering short answer questions, to learning to organize information through writing a resume and business letter. Students then progress to writing narrative, persuasive essays, and process essays. In the research component, students learn to use the library, to take notes, to develop a bibliography, and to prepare an annotated essay using parenthetical footnotes. The final section includes a mini research paper, a debate on a research topic, and a research paper.

We suggest that teachers begin the research-paper project early in the course, so that students have ample time to do research. We often have students choose topics by the third week of the course. Please refer to the beginning of the research-paper project for additional information.

The underlying philosophy of *Writing Your Way* is that, because people are different, they have preferred styles of learning. Through interactive exercises in a workshop setting, students gain insight into the communication process. Once they have experimented with communication, they are able to write with greater ease.

AUDIENCE

By introducing the concept of audience, *Writing Your Way* allows students to become critical listeners as well as critical writers. Through the first exercise in which students give oral directions and observe how another interprets what they say, students see what happens when communication, either written or spoken, is unclear. From this, they establish certain guidelines that help to clarify communication.

In *Writing Your Way*, students are given the tools to understand what is required to communicate an idea. In this text, students consider the audience (the reader). In the first chapter, they deal with the concept of audience through a simple interactive exercise; however, by the end of the book, they must present the information they have gathered for their research paper in a debate. Here, they get a true sense of audience and how different people interpret and use information.

WRITING MATRIX

Writing Your Way introduces the concept of the *writing matrix*, a simple device to help students sort their ideas and determine the value of their supporting information. Students who like to jot down ideas before they write can use the visual device of the matrix to be sure they have supporting information for each of their ideas. Students who prefer to begin an essay by writing and to see what develops can use the matrix as a way to check that each main idea is supported adequately. This visual representation of the essay is a valuable tool in developing clear, effective writing. The matrix can be used either before or after writing to plan and test the strength of the essay.

LIBRARY AND RESEARCH WRITING TECHNIQUES

Writing Your Way encourages students to do library research and teaches students research techniques prior to writing. Students learn to use the library and how to take notes, quote, summarize, paraphrase, and incorporate this information into the body of the research paper.

A unique feature of *Writing Your Way* is a section on incorporating quoted material. Most students use the expression, "so and so said. . . ." In this chapter, students learn how to include quotations. They learn to use brackets and ellipsis marks and to create a smooth transition between their words and those of the quoted source.

MINI RESEARCH PAPER

Often, students must write a lengthy research paper without ever being given the opportunity to practice the art of research paper writing. In *Writing Your Way*, after students have learned how to write parenthetical footnotes and a bibliography, they are given a short annotated essay or mini-research paper to write. The research material is provided in the text in the form of two readings. Students read them, take notes, establish their purpose or point, and write a correctly documented *mini research paper* or annotated essay. Papers can then be reviewed to make sure students have learned to take notes, to give credit, and to cite sources correctly. Once students have had this experience, they have a better understanding of the more complicated task of doing independent research and writing a research paper.

DEBATE

A unique feature of *Writing Your Way* is the use of an in-class debate as part of the research project. Through the debate, students have the opportunity to test their information and to hear the arguments or criticism a listener may have. The debate allows students to analyze both sides of their topic. It provides students with a forum to test their ideas and the adequacy of their documentation. This aspect is often lacking in writing classes.

The debate also gives students the opportunity to present their ideas verbally so they can evaluate themselves as speakers and gain confidence as presenters. Through the debate, students gain insight into the dynamics of communication and internalize much of the information they have gathered. By the time they are ready to write their research papers, they are extremely familiar with their topics and better able to present them in a coherent, logical manner.

We usually devote three 50-minute class periods to the debate. Each student has a minimum of 3 minutes and a maximum of 4 minutes to present his or her information. When time is allowed for writing the proposition on the board, with the names of the affirmative and negative team members, and for voting to determine the influence the debate has had on the audience, each proposition will require approximately 25 minutes. Some classes become very interested in the topic and have questions to ask the debaters after the debate. If you expect to include this type of discussion, allow more time for the debate.

SAMPLE RESEARCH PAPER

Because each teacher has a special method of grading essays, we suggest that you grade and comment on the sample research paper at the end of the book, then copy it and discuss it with your students. In this way, they will understand what you are looking for and how you grade papers. Another approach is to assign sections of the sample research paper to the class to edit, proofread, and/or rewrite.

WRITING YOUR WAY EVALUATION SUMMARY FORM

ASSIGNMENTS

	Resume	Rewrite	Cover Letter	Rewrite	Short Answers	Short Answers	Short Answers	Essay	Essay	Narrative	Rewrite	Persuasion	Rewrite	Process	Rewrite	Mini research
Content																
Organization																
Attention-Getter							✓									
Purpose					✓		✓	✓								
Topic Sentence																
Introduction		✓					✓									
Background Information																
Supporting Information																
Transitions																
Conclusion		✓					✓									
Sentence Structure																
Fragments		✓			✓											
Run-Ons																
Choppy Sentences							✓									
Wordy Sentences																
Misplaced Modifiers																
Subject/Verb Agreement																
Other																
Verbs																
Verb Forms																
Verb Tense		✓			✓											
Infinitives																
Passive/Active Voice																
Other																
Language																
Dictionary																
Thesaurus																
Spelling	✓	✓			✓	✓	✓	✓								
Word Forms	✓															
Redundant Wording																
Nonspecific Language																
Misused Words																
Articles	✓	✓						✓								
Pronoun Use																
Other																
Punctuation																
Comma																
Apostrophe																
Colon/Semicolon																
Other																
Editing						✓	✓									
Proofreading							✓									

Note: When your teacher returns the Evaluation Form, enter the information on this page. This will help you keep track of the areas you have improved in and those that need work.

To the Student

Every year, students enter college freshman composition courses worried about their English. They are unhappy that they are going to have to write because they dislike writing.

This book was written for all those students who dislike writing. In this book you will discover that your thoughts are important and that writing is simply another way of expressing yourself. In fact, the only difference between the two is that writing is more exact. People can read your document several times: they can examine it because it doesn't disappear into air as spoken words do. You don't have the opportunity to watch people's faces to see if they understand or to answer their questions. Your document stands by itself.

This is no reason to fear writing. As long as you have something to say—this is the key element—people will want to read what you have written.

Therefore, the first rule of good writing is to have something important to say. This may be an idea, a feeling, a position, a fact, or an opinion. However, it must be something that is important. Your thoughts, feelings, and beliefs are valuable and important.

Once you have learned that, you will find that writing is an interesting process. It may help you to think through an idea. It may give you the opportunity to express your feelings, permit you to document your research, to explain how well you have learned a lesson, or to give directions to another.

In this book, you will work on some exciting assignments to help you to understand what a reader expects from you, the author. You will learn a technique for answering short answer essay test questions and to prepare a matrix to help you think through and organize your material. You will also write a mini research paper so that you will know all the steps of writing a research paper. Finally, with your classmates, you will work on a research project which includes a debate. Then you will write the research paper.

We hope that you will enjoy the workshop approach of this book and that you will complete your writing course with greater confidence in your ability as a writer.

Introduction

So often, students say, "I'm going to be an engineer, or a computer scientist. Why do I need to learn how to write?" If you feel this way about learning to write, perhaps the letter and response below will help you understand the importance of writing well.

Q: I'm a very good engineer but I write miserably. Will this hurt my career? If so, what can I do about it?

A: Sorry, but it will hurt your career. A recent MIT study found that engineers, managers, and supervisors spend from a third to half their time writing, reading, and speaking and that their career success is related to how well they communicate. Whatever your engineering competence, you must be able to write clearly to have influence and success.

Here's a way to begin to improve. First, it's not enough to know you're a "miserable" writer: you must understand your specific problems. Do you have trouble organizing? Are your sentences too long and clumsy? Do you use words that are too long and technical or too vague to be understood? Determine your weaknesses.

Once you know what you need to learn, seek out a course or a private instructor to help you. It's also essential to have the best references handy. Buy copies of a good dictionary and good writing handbook: I prefer *Elements of Style* by W. Strunk Jr. and E. B. White (Macmillan paperback, 1979).

Source: Phyllis Mindell, "Communication: Improving Concentration, Making Business Meetings More Productive, Improving Writing Skills," *Rochester Business Magazine*, vol. 3 (1986), p. 5.

Another common complaint is, "I'm an international student. When I return to my home country, I won't need English." Here are several responses to this comment:

1. If you get a degree from an English-speaking institution, you are expected to have a good command of the language. People in your home country may ask you to prepare letters for international correspondence or to interpret or translate. Poor English skills could be embarrassing to you and to others.
2. If you decide to gain work experience in an English-speaking country, good English competency will be helpful to you and to your employer.

Can you think of other reasons for learning to write well?

_____

_____

_____

_____

_____

_____

_____

Writing Assessment

So that you and your instructor can assess your writing strengths and areas for improvement, write a 500-word essay on a topic of your choice. Your instructor will evaluate it using the Writing Evaluation Form. See page 225. This will help you track your progress and will contain assignments from the "Error Correction/Reference Section" (Chapter 11) which relate directly to your writing needs.

You may choose one of the topics listed below or from those provided by your instructor.

1. Attending college in a foreign country is beneficial. Provide reasons and examples.
2. Individuals should (or should not) be allowed to own handguns. Provide reasons and examples.
3. Citizens should (should not) be required to vote in national elections. Provide reasons and examples.
4. If I could change one thing about my country, it would be _____ because _____ .
5. Which is more important for success: intelligence or common sense? Why?
6. What is the most important thing you have learned from your family? Give examples of how this will benefit you in the future.
7. If you won a million dollars, how would you spend it? Give reasons and examples.
8. What qualities would you seek in choosing a person to marry? Provide details and examples.

The purpose of this first essay is for evaluation purposes only. Your teacher will return the essay to you with a completed evaluation form indicating your strengths and weaknesses in writing. Enter the information from the evaluation form on the summary form at the back of your book and complete any special assignments your instructor may have suggested.

Your instructor may want to collect these essays and hold them until the last day of class so that you can see the progess that you have made over the course of the term.

One

Presenting Information as the Reader Expects to Read It

One of the most confusing aspects of writing is determining the best way to present material so that the reader can understand it. So often, because *we* know what we want to say, we assume that the reader knows it also. However, the reader will *not* know what you mean unless you express your point clearly. The cartoon below demonstrates what can happen when two people have different expectations and points of view.

Source: HAGAR © 1988 King Features Syndicate, Inc. Reprinted with special permission of King Features Syndicate, Inc.

Knowing Your Audience

The writer must know his or her audience and be prepared to answer questions that readers may have. Often, when we write and speak, we assume our audience knows what we know. If we are speaking with people, we can tell by their expression if they understand us. However, because our reader must rely solely on what we have written, we must be especially careful to analyze our reader's needs and to provide clear, concise information.

EXPERIMENTING WITH COMMUNICATION

Let us try an experiment to see how well you can communicate without knowing whether your listener understands you.

Do the Following:

1. Cut out the puzzle pieces on the opposite page. (You may trace them onto a separate paper if you do not wish to cut the page.)
2. Choose a partner.
3. Sit back to back.
4. One person should construct a picture or design using the pieces. Then he or she must tell the other student how to construct the picture or design, but may not look to see if his or her partner has put the puzzle together correctly.
5. The person who has the puzzle may not ask questions but must follow the directions given by his or her partner exactly.
6. When you have solved the puzzle, raise your hand.
7. You have 10 minutes to complete the puzzle.

Checking Your Solution:

After 10 minutes, your teacher will direct the person giving the directions to look at what his or her partner has done. If the puzzle is the same as the solution, you are to be congratulated. If it is not, you may continue to give instructions to your partner—but this time you may watch to see how your partner follows your directions.

Questions:

When you have finished this experiment, answer the following questions:

People Solving the Puzzle:

1. How did you feel while you were trying to solve the puzzle?
2. What problems did you have when you were receiving directions?
3. What should your partner have done differently?
4. What should you have done differently?

5

People Giving Directions:

1. How did you feel while you were giving directions?
2. What problems did you have when you were giving directions?
3. What do you think caused the problem in communication?
4. What would you have done differently?
5. Would it have helped to know what you were making from the beginning? Why?

Now switch roles so that the person who followed directions will give directions. However, before you begin, consider what the result would be if you:

1. Told the person what he or she will be constructing.
2. Numbered the puzzle pieces and told how many there were in your picture.

Now, reverse roles. You have 10 minutes to give directions.

Debriefing:

Most of us assume that other people know what we know. When we speak, we can watch the other person's expression to determine if he or she understands. The other person can also ask us questions about what we mean. However, when we write, we must be very clear, because the reader cannot ask us for verification and we cannot see the reader's expression.

From this experiment, you should have learned the importance of immediately telling the listener what you are talking about or what the point is. This way, the reader understands your purpose from the beginning.

NOW YOU DO IT

Now that you understand the importance of explaining things clearly, try the following exercises. Remember to include all necessary information and to write the steps in the proper sequence.

1. Each student should hide something in the classroom and write directions for someone to find it. Then give the directions to a classmate, who must actually locate the object.
2. Write directions for doing one of the following:
    a. Making a book cover from a paper bag
    b. Wrapping a present
    c. Using a yo-yo
    d. Making a paper airplane
    e. Tying shoelaces
   When you have finished, exchange papers and have a student read the directions aloud while a third student follows them *exactly* as they are written.

Understanding Writing Patterns

Different countries have different methods for organizing material. For instance, Robert Kaplan categorizes writing from different parts of the world by using the diagrams below:

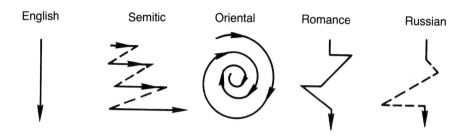

Source: Robert Kaplan, "Cultural Thought Patterns in Intercultural Education," *Language Learning*, 1966, vol. 15, no. 1, 2, p. 15. Reprinted with permission of Robert Kaplan and Language Learning.

These drawings indicate that in English, the writer says this is my point, this is why I believe this way, or here is my proof and my examples. All the information in a piece of writing in English will relate directly to the point. Writers from other parts of the world are not so direct and are careful not to sound as though they know all the answers. Some hint at or suggest what they believe. Others present all information as having equal value.

In Semitic writing, the ideas are presented parallel to one another without making any one idea more important than another. Oriental writing tends to be circular. The author speaks around the ideas, making suggestions but not bluntly expressing the point. In both Romance languages (Italian, Spanish, and French) and Russian, writers tend to digress a great deal. However, in academic writing in English, you must remember to be direct, to state your purpose, and then to substantiate it with relevant details or examples.

Getting to the Point

In English, the key to good academic and business writing is telling the reader, as soon as possible, exactly what you mean. Generally, the author states the main idea or point in one sentence. If the author is writing an essay, the idea the author wants to present is stated in one sentence, called the *thesis sentence*. This sentence appears in the introduction or first paragraph. Its purpose is to express the writer's reason for writing and to provide a focus for the ideas expressed in the essay.

Each paragraph the writer develops thereafter to support or prove the thesis sentence has a *topic sentence*. This sentence tells the reader what the paragraph will be about. Each sentence in the paragraph must support that topic sentence.

Look at the first draft of an introductory paragraph below:

> Strict parents are not always the most popular people in the minds of children. There are many positive traits that are found in children from strict households.

Consider these questions:

1. Do you know what the essay will be about?
2. Do you have enough background information to understand the topic?
3. Do you know what the author's position is?
4. The essay was written in response to a topic given in an English composition class. What do you think the topic was?

Now look at the second draft of this introductory paragraph. How has the writer changed it?

> My parents are too strict! This is a common saying among teenagers. Although students don't realize it at the time, the stricter parents are, the better their children are in the long run. This is true because strict parents raise children who have good manners, are respectful, and have good study habits.

Consider these questions:

1. What is your reaction to this revised introductory paragraph?
2. Which do you like better? Why?
3. What information in this paragraph do you think the writer will develop or explain?
4. Can you figure out what question or topic the professor gave the class to write about?

In the revised paragraph, one of the areas the writer talks about is good manners. The reader can expect this subject to be the focus of one paragraph. In this paragraph, the writer will use examples to prove that children of strict parents do have good manners.

What else does the writer discuss? The writer discusses being respectful and having good study habits. Because these are two different ideas, each will require its own paragraph.

If you were the author of this essay, what examples could you use to support the idea that strict parents encourage good study habits in their children? What do they tell their children to do?

1. _____

2. _____

3. _____

4. _____

How did your parents encourage you to have good study habits?

1. _____

2. _____

3. _____

4. _____

How does this make strict parents better? Write a sentence that states that. Now write a paragraph following this order:

1. Write one sentence that tells the reader that strict parents are better parents because they encourage good study habits in their children.
2. Write three or four sentences that give examples of how strict parents encourage good study habits. Use the information you provided above.
3. Write a sentence that tells why you think this is good and, therefore, why this makes strict parents better parents.

When you combine these sentences, you will have a paragraph to support the idea that strict parents teach good study habits and, therefore, are better than parents who are not strict.

Look at the paragraph below, which one student developed to support this idea:

> Strict parents tend to teach and to enforce good study habits. My parents made me study from seven to nine on Sunday through Thursday nights. As a result, now that I am in college and independent, I tend to follow the same study pattern. In addition, my parents never allowed me to study with the radio or television on. At the time, I thought these rules were ridiculous, but now I recognize the wisdom of my parents.

Here is an example of a paragraph a student wrote to support the idea that strict parents make better parents because they teach children good manners:

> One thing that children learn from strict parents is good manners. My parents were very strict with me. They insisted that I use my silverware correctly and that I never speak with food in my mouth. They taught me to be respectful to my elders and always address them with a title such as Miss, Mr., or Mrs. Now that I am older, I appreciate the effort that my parents made to teach me good manners. I know that I make a good impression when I am with people, and I feel very comfortable knowing that good manners are an integral part of me.

NOW YOU DO IT

Write a paragraph of your own to support the idea that strict parents teach children good manners. The questions we used earlier were meant to guide you so that you would understand the concept of the American paragraph. The American paragraph is linear in development, which contrasts with the way in which other cultures present their ideas and information. The essay on the next page is a graphic presentation of the way a linear essay is written.

Other Topics to Develop

Write your opinion on one or more of the topics listed below. Keep in mind that you must present information directly to the reader. Do not limit your ideas to one paragraph.

1. Cartoons teach children to accept violence.
2. There are too many violent movies and television shows.
3. International students should pay full tuition at American universities.
4. There should be no drinking-age limit in the United States.
5. Euthanasia should be legalized.
6. People should use birth control to limit the number of children they have.
7. Governments should control the number of children that families can have.
8. Other topic of your choice.

Sequence of Paragraphs

The sequence of paragraphs on the following page represents an overview of the format used in an essay. It is an example of how a writer might sequence paragraphs to demonstrate why strict parents are better than parents who are not strict. Notice that each idea presented in the introduction is developed in one of the body paragraphs. Over the next few chapters we will look at the various components of the essay.

My parents are too strict! This is a common saying among teenagers. Although students don't realize it at the time, the stricter their parents are, the better their children are in the long run. This is true because strict parents raise children who have good manners, are respectful, and have good study habits.

One thing that children learn from strict parents is good manners. My parents were very strict with me. They insisted that I use my silverware correctly, that I never speak with food in my mouth. I know that I make a good impression when I am with people and I feel very comfortable knowing that good manners are an integral part of me.

Strict parents tend to teach and enforce good study habits. My parents made me study from seven to nine on Sunday through Thursday nights. As a result, now that I am in college and independent I tend to follow the same study pattern. In addition, my parents never allowed me to study with the radio or television on. At the time I thought these rules were ridiculous, but now I recognize the wisdom of my parents.

My parents also taught me to be respectful. The golden rule to "Do unto others as you would have them do unto you" was emphasized at my house. I always stand to give my seat to an older person. I address them with a title such as Miss, Mr., or Mrs. I am comfortable putting my hand out to shake hands to greet people and I have learned through the years always to be polite. Now that I am older, I appreciate the effort my parents made to teach me good manners.

In the 1980s children have become more independent and knowledgeable from watching television and being exposed to many things. But exposure and knowledge of information are no substitute for the rules and regulations that parents set for making children pleasant, respectful, and contributing members of society.

NOW YOU DO IT

Look at your writing from the preceding page and see if it has this element of development.

Two
Paragraph Organization

Topic Sentences

As you learned in Chapter 1, an American paragraph has a particular order. First, it contains a *topic sentence*. This sentence tells the reader what the paragraph is about. Examine the following *topic* and possible *topic sentences* and write what you think the paragraph will be about.

Topic: *College Entrance Examinations.*

Topic Sentences:

1. College entrance examinations cannot always predict whether a student will succeed in college.

   _____

   _____

2. Because college entrance examinations are so important, many students attend special courses to prepare for them.

   _____

   _____

3. College entrance examinations primarily measure the student's mathematical ability and reading comprehension.

   _____

   _____

NOW YOU DO IT

To check your understanding of topics and topic sentences, put a **T** next to the *topics* and **TS** in front of the *topic sentences:*

———— 1. Gun control.

———— 2. Only law enforcement officials should be allowed to carry handguns.

———— 3. Euthanasia.

———— 4. Euthanasia should be allowed if the patient is mentally competent and requests that he or she be allowed to die.

———— 5. The 55-mile-per-hour speed limit in the United States.

———— 6. The United States should have unlimited speeds on interstate highways.

Before you continue, have your instructor check your work.

Now that you see how topic sentences are constructed, develop two topic sentences for each topic.

Topic: *Attending College.*

Topic Sentences:

_____

_____

_____

_____

Topic: *Choosing a College.*

Topic Sentences:

_____

_____

_____

_____

Topic: *Succeeding at College.*

Topic Sentences:

_____

_____

_____

_____

When you have finished, share your topic sentences with the class. Notice how many different ways you can approach a topic. The topic sentence provides the direction your writing will take.

Body Sentences

The *body sentences* come after the *topic sentence*. These sentences support the topic sentence by giving relevant details, reasons, or examples. These must be directly related to the topic sentence.

Read the topic sentence below and circle the body sentences that directly support the topic sentence:

Topic: *Benefits of Working One's Way Through College.*

Topic Sentence: *Students receive many benefits by working their way through college.*

Body Sentences:

1. Because they must balance work and study, students learn to manage their time more effectively.
2. Working can keep a student from attending extracurricular activities.
3. Jobs provide valuable employment experience, which can be an asset upon graduation.
4. Students who pay their own tuition tend to achieve higher grades and to take their education more seriously.
5. A working student does not have time to take courses that are not directly related to his major.

Sentences 1, 3, and 4 show the advantages of working and, therefore, relate directly to the topic sentence. Sentences 2 and 5 are disadvantages. They do not support the topic and should not be included in the paragraph.

If your topic was to discuss the disadvantages of working one's way through college, what body sentences might you include?

1. _____
2. _____
3. _____
4. _____

Development Types

There are many ways to develop your paragraph. Two of the most common are *development by example* and *development by supporting details*. Look at each sample paragraph below and notice how information is used to develop the *topic sentence*.

DEVELOPMENT BY EXAMPLE (paragraph A)

Older people should not be forced to retire because of their age. In 1985, I began working at Komton Auto Parts Factory. An older employee showed me what to do and helped me keep pace with the assembly line. He also shared his experiences with me. If it hadn't been for him, I would not have been able to learn the job as quickly and handle it as effectively.

DEVELOPMENT BY SUPPORTING DETAILS (paragraph B)

Computers are replacing typewriters in the office. Employees who do know how to type can enter documents directly on the computer without secretarial assistance. Documents can be edited or reformatted easily. Multiple copies can be made with the flick of a switch.

Audience Exercise:

How we select the details and examples we use depends on the audience. Suppose you were writing paragraph B for an organization of senior citizens. How would the paragraph be different?

NOW YOU DO IT

Choose three topic sentences from the ones you developed in the "Now You Do It" exercise on page 14. Develop three or four *body sentences* for each. Make certain that each sentence provides specific reasons, details, or examples to support your *topic sentence*.

Topic Sentence: _____
_____

Body Sentences:

1. _____
2. _____
3. _____
4. _____

Topic Sentence: _____
_____

16

Body Sentences:

1. _____

2. _____

3. _____

4. _____

Topic Sentence: _____

_____

Body Sentences:

1. _____

2. _____

3. _____

4. _____

Concluding Sentence

The last sentence of a paragraph is the *concluding sentence.* This sentence pulls the paragraph together and indicates that you have proven your point. It can summarize the content, make a closing statement, or ask the reader to take a particular action. Some writers even ask a final question which is directly related to the contents of the paragraph.

Examine the following paragraph and determine what the concluding sentence does:

> People complain about politicians, but they never do anything about them! [*attention-getting sentence*] However, instead of complaining to your friends, you can do several things to let your political representatives know your opinion. [*topic sentence*] First, you can inform your senator or congressman about your stance and suggestions by writing a well-planned, specific letter. Second, you can join a political action group that lobbies for specific reforms or issues. This will unite your voice with many and increase your chances for success. Finally, you can vote. This is often your most powerful weapon because even one vote can decide an election—and your congressman knows it. [*body sentences*] Now, aren't any of these alternatives a great deal more effective and satisfying than griping? [*concluding sentence*]

As you can see, the *concluding sentence* summarizes the results of the alternatives given in the *body sentences* and asks the reader to make a decision.

NOW YOU DO IT

Write a *concluding sentence* for each of the *topic-sentence* and *body-sentence* units you developed in the "Now You Do It" exercise on page 16.

Concluding Sentence: _____

_____

Concluding Sentence: _____

_____

Concluding Sentence: _____

_____

The Attention-Getting Sentence

A paragraph, if it is the first one in an essay or must stand alone, may also contain an *attention-getting sentence*. The attention-getting sentence can be one of the following:

1. A question
2. A controversial or thought-provoking statement
3. A quotation
4. A one-line joke
5. A statement of fact

The *attention-getting sentence* must be related directly to the *topic sentence*, however.

Here is an example of a paragraph with an attention-getting sentence:

> What is worth an average of $25 million and is given away free? [*attention-getting sentence*] The Rochester Telephone Company's Yellow Pages, which are distributed free to consumers, contain over $25 million dollars worth of advertisements and hundreds of dollars of free coupons. [*topic sentence*] The advertisements help consumers locate businesses, services, or agencies from "Abrasives" to "Zoos." Customers can use the Yellow Pages coupons for items ranging from free hamburgers from Burger King to $100 rebates from Wal-Rae Heating and Cooling, Inc. [*body sentences*] No wonder people look forward to the delivery of the Rochester Telephone Company's Yellow Pages. [*concluding sentence*]

Notice that the *attention-getting sentence* arouses your curiosity. The *topic sentence* tells what the paragraph is about. The *body sentences* supply specific details to support the topic sentence. The *concluding sentence* makes a final statement to unite the content of the paragraph.

NOW YOU DO IT

Try writing an attention-getting sentence for the paragraph below. Think of a question, quotation, one-line joke, or controversial statement that will get the reader's attention. When you have written your sentence, your instructor will ask you to share it with the class.

_____

_____

_____[attention-getting sentence]

Living in a college dormitory has many financial advantages. [*topic sentence*] First, dorm-room rent is usually about half the cost of an off-campus apartment. Second, because dormitory rooms are completely furnished and include maid and linen service, students can save money on cleaning supplies and on household furnishings necessary for an apartment. Finally, dorm rent includes utilities, which can be as much as $300 per month in an apartment. [*body sentences*] For the student on a limited budget, dorm living provides an excellent financial incentive. [*concluding sentence*]

NOW YOU DO IT

Now that you have had the opportunity to develop an attention-getting sentence for a sample paragraph and have heard the attention-getting sentences written by your classmates, it is time to develop attention-getting sentences for your own paragraphs.

1. Choose one of the topic/body/concluding sentence groups you developed in the "Now You Do It" exercise on page 16. Combine these sentences into a paragraph and develop an *attention-getting sentence* to add interest to your writing. After you have completed this assignment, have your instructor check your work. Then share your paragraph with the class.
2. The instructor will divide the class into groups of five or six students. Exchange paragraphs with each other and write an attention-getting sentence for each paragraph.

NOW YOU DO IT

Even more fun than developing a paragraph on your own is developing one with a group. In this exercise, you will see how sentences are written to form a cohesive paragraph. Make sure each sentence you develop relates directly to the topic sentence.

1. On a sheet of notebook paper, write a *topic sentence.* Then pass your paper to the person beside you.
2. This person will write one *body sentence* to support the *topic sentence.* Then he or she passes the paper to third and fourth students who also write *body sentences.* The fourth student passes the paper to a fifth student. Remember, each body sentence must relate directly to the topic sentence.
3. The fifth student must read the paragraph and write a *concluding sentence.* He or she then passes the paragraph to a sixth student.
4. The sixth student adds an *attention-getting sentence* to the beginning of the paragraph and passes the paragraph to a seventh student.
5. The seventh student reads the paragraph carefully to make certain the attention-getting, body, and concluding sentences relate directly to the topic sentence. The student also checks the paragraph for grammar and spelling.

When you have finished, be prepared to read your group's paragraph aloud. Every student will have the opportunity to provide a topic sentence; to write an attention-getting, body, and concluding sentence; and to check paragraphs for coherence.

Note: If you have done this properly, each sentence will support the topic sentence and the paragraph will present an idea in a clear fashion.

Think about how you decided what your sentence would say. If you were writing a body sentence, you had to read the other sentences and add another piece of information. If you were writing the attention-getting sentence, you had to read the entire paragraph and come up with an interesting way to introduce the subject. If you were writing the conclusion, you had to write a sentence that brought closure, made a statement, or gave the audience something to think about in the future.

Three
Business and Professional Writing

A high school senior was applying for admission to ten colleges. One day his teacher asked how he was coming along with his applications. He responded that he had filled them out. His teacher was surprised and pleased. She asked when he had mailed them in. "Oh," he said, "I haven't mailed them yet. I still have to write all the essays!"

This story is true for many students. They fill in their name, address, telephone number, and grades and then sit and stare at a blank piece of paper.

Many students freeze when they have to fill out a college application, write a resume, apply for a scholarship, or write any type of formal letter. In this chapter, you will learn the basic formula for doing these types of writing.

The purpose of this chapter is not only to teach you to write a business letter and resume but to show you the tools you can use to organize your writing. This information will be particularly useful when you organize your research paper.

Source: Jim Davis, *Garfield.* © 1988 United Features Syndicate, Inc.

Writing the Resume

One of the most effective ways to learn to organize and to write well is through business correspondence. Writing the resume forces the writer to analyze, to summarize, and to organize material effectively. The writer must also examine his material from the reader's point of view (which in this case is the employer). In this way, the writer can prepare the resume to meet specific job qualifications in order to encourage the employer to consider the applicant for the position. In the first chapter, we talked about the importance of the audience. Now we will put that information to use.

Therefore, in this chapter, we will practice what we have previously learned: to analyze, organize, and summarize our information for the reader.

THE PURPOSE AND CONTENT OF THE RESUME

The resume is a brief summary of a job applicant's education, work history, and special abilities or awards. To determine the content of the resume, you must analyze the requirements of the job you are applying for and consider your audience. This is the same method you use when you determine the content of an essay or a short essay question.

RESUME	ESSAY QUESTION
What's the job? What does it require? What topics should I include? What details should I include?	What's the question? What information is required? What topics should I include? What details and examples should I include?
Who's the audience? What does the reader already know? What is expected? What does the reader want to know? How should I organize my material to make sure the reader gets the point?	Who's the audience? What does the reader already know? What is expected? What does the reader want to know? How should I organize my material to make sure the reader gets the point?

Although the form of the resume may vary, a resume usually contains the following:

1. Your name, address, and telephone number
2. Your job objective: This is the type of job that you are seeking
3. Your educational background: This includes where you went to college, your major, the dates you attended, the degree you received. You may also include your grade point average and a summary of your courses.
4. Your job history: This includes your job title, the company and address, dates of employment, and a specific listing of your job responsibilities.
5. Other important information:
   Languages you speak
   Machine or programming languages you know well
   Certificates or licenses in job-related areas
   Honors you have received
   Memberships and offices in clubs or professional organizations
   Special interests or hobbies

On the following pages are examples of resumes. Notice the format. The most recent information is always presented first. The resume always begins with the job objective, which clearly states what type of job the applicant is seeking. This helps the employer determine whether you are looking for the job he is offering. Resumes should be easy to read and presented in such a fashion that a busy employer can quickly locate the important information. (Remember to keep the audience in mind.) The resume should be neat, typed, and well spaced on the page for easy reading. A visually attractive resume creates a positive first impression.

BEING THE AUDIENCE

Because it is so important to write for an audience, in this exercise, you will have the opportunity to switch roles and be the audience (employer).

You will review the resumes of the applicants who have applied for a position to teach English as a second language at a college. This means the person will be teaching English to non-native speakers of English.

Break up into groups of seven or eight students. Analyze the resumes and, as a group, decide whom you would hire and why. Also decide why you would not hire some of the applicants.

Before you begin, here is some information that may help you in your decision:

1. Most schools like to hire teachers who have a master's degree in TESOL (M.A. TESOL).
2. Prior teaching experience is important.
3. ESL stands for English as a second language.
4. Preference is often given to people who demonstrate competency in another language or who have lived or taught in a foreign country.
5. Publications relating to teaching are evidence of scholarship.

Rules:

1. You will have 15 minutes to agree on a candidate and prepare a list of reasons why you have chosen this person. Everyone in the group must agree. If someone doesn't agree with your choice, it is up to you to convince that person that your applicant is the best.
2. Appoint a recorder, who will write down the reasons why the group has selected a particular candidate.
3. One person from each group will tell the class which applicant the group selected and why.

Now you are ready to begin.

RESUME

JOHN HENTLEY

347 ASHTON DRIVE   263 COVINGTON DRIVE
ROCHESTER, NY 14618   BOCA RATON, FL 33433
(716) 345-6678   (305) 347-7890

JOB OBJECTIVE: Position as ESL instructor in a junior
                   college or university.

WORK EXPERIENCE:

1986–1987   TEACHER OF ENGLISH AS A SECOND
              LANGUAGE,
              Orland High School, Midtown, IA

              Taught conversation and grammar courses for
              ninth- and tenth-grade students.

1980–1986   ATHLETIC DIRECTOR FOR A HEALTH SPA
              Athletic Lady Health Spa, Little Rock, AR

              Managed athletic program for 500-client health
              spa, developed physical fitness programs,
              designed educational programs for cardiac
              patients, directed and trained physical fitness
              instructors.

1978–1982   TENNIS PROFESSIONAL
              Midlakes Tennis Club, Lakeville, MA

              Taught tennis at beginning, intermediate, and
              advanced levels.

EDUCATION:

1977   B.A. from Yale University in Physical Education

1978   M.A. from Columbia University in Secondary Education
         Program Design

LANGUAGES:

Fluent in French, Italian, Russian, Spanish, and Polish

SPECIAL INTERESTS:

Tennis, languages, travel

REFERENCES AVAILABLE UPON REQUEST

JUDITH MULSON
567 BELMONT AVE.
WEBSTER, NY 14580
(716) 872-3389

JOB OBJECTIVE: To teach English as a second language

EDUCATION:

1986   M.A. TESOL, University of Rochester
1982   B.A. University of Rochester

EXPERIENCE:

1986—present   ESL instructor, Rochester Institute of
                 Technology, Rochester, NY.

                 Presently teaching conversation, grammar, and
                 composition classes for international students
                 in the basic and intermediate levels. Working
                 in learning lab on a one-to-one basis with
                 students in pronunciation and writing.
                 Responsible for design of class materials.

1985—1986   Private tutor of English to nonnative speakers
                 of English, Rochester, NY.

                 Provided individual instruction to nonnative
                 speakers and developed individualized study
                 programs. Most students were at the basic
                 level and required extensive instruction in
                 grammar and pronunciation.

1985   English teacher, Loman High School, Barwick,
                 NJ.

                 Permanent substitute teacher in ninth- and
                 twelfth-grade literature classes.

1982—1985   Peace Corps volunteer in Africa.

LANGUAGES: Swahili and some Yoruba

REFERENCES AVAILABLE UPON REQUEST

Susan Tuttle
367 Andersonville Avenue
Ithaca, NY 14580
(607) 277-6789

JOB OBJECTIVE: To be a program administrator of an
                   English as a second language program

EXPERIENCE:

1987–present   Instructor in ESOL program at University of
                   Buffalo, Buffalo, NY

                   Responsible for conversation, pronunciation,
                   and writing courses for advanced-level
                   students. Presently in charge of language
                   laboratory and tutoring program.

1986–1987   Instructor of ESOL at Oneonta State University
                   of New York at Oneonta

                   Taught beginning conversation and grammar
                   to nonnative speakers. Worked extensively in
                   laboratory and tutoring programs. Designed
                   student handbooks for grammar and writing
                   workshops presented by ESOL department.

1983–1986   Instructor at the University of California,
                   Berkeley, teaching English composition

                   Taught English composition to both advanced
                   and basic English classes. Worked in English
                   Writing Lab and designed self-instructional
                   materials in writing.

1982–1983   Instructor of high school English, Honeoye, NY
                   Taught eleventh- and twelfth-grade literature.

EDUCATION: Ph.D. University of Kentucky, TESOL
                   M.A.   University of Florida, Education
                   B.A.   City College of New York, English

HONORS: Phi Beta Kappa National Honor Society

ARTICLES PUBLISHED:

"Error Correction in Writing" in the *TESOL Quarterly*, 1987

REFERENCES AVAILABLE UPON REQUEST

1. Each group recorder should report to the class which candidate the group selected and the reasons the candidate was chosen.
2. After each group has spoken, discuss as a whole the class's reaction to the various resumes. Some things to consider are:
   a. Appearance
   b. Format
   c. Content
   d. Organization
   e. Sense of the person (what you think this person is like)
   f. Educational experience
   g. Work experience

Notice that *appearance* is placed first. When an envelope is opened, the first thing one sees is the overall appearance of the documents. If the resume is unpresentable, the employer will probably throw it in the wastepaper basket! If this happens, the employer will never get to read about the experiences the applicant has had.

Consider what you thought about and what was important to you when you were the audience, or employer, in the last exercise. List some of the information you considered when deciding to accept or reject an applicant:

1. _____
2. _____
3. _____
4. _____
5. _____

WRITING YOUR RESUME

Before you can write a resume, you must first decide what type of job you are seeking. Begin by getting a copy of the classified advertisements from your local newspaper or a copy of a job posting from your college placement office. Read the advertisements carefully and select a job which you would like to have now or one which you will be qualified for when you complete your schooling.

Remember that the *job objective* should state the job you wish to have. If you are applying for a position in the newspaper or at a placement agency, word your job objective exactly like the job posting.

Write your job objective here:

_____

_____

_____

Next, consider all the information that you can include in your resume. Using index cards, (3″ × 5″ cards are best) write each piece of information about the following topics on a separate card. Be sure to include dates where applicable.

Work experience (include the dates you worked, your employer, and your job responsibilities)

Languages you are fluent in

Education (degrees, school, years attended)

Travel

Honors you have received (athletic, social, or academic)

Publications or exhibitions of your work

Some examples would be:

1987   B.A. ESOL, Oxford University

Fluent in French and Japanese

1986–1987   Spanish Tutor, University of Toledo

Tutored Spanish to beginning and intermediate graduate and
undergrad students in the Foreign Language Program.

Working knowledge of Lotus 3, Multiplan, WordStar, and Cobal.

After you have filled out your index cards, sort them by categories. Sort each packet of cards by placing the *most recent* information first. When all the cards are sorted in descending order by dates within each category, you are ready to write your resume.

Determine what you want your resume to look like. Where do you want your name and address? Do you have both a permanent address and a school address? Do you want to use both? Think about where it will be the easiest for the employer to locate you if he or she wants to write or to call.

If a typewriter or computer is available to you, type your resume. You will be very pleased at the way it looks. Keep your resume handy so you can use it when you apply for a job. As you acquire more skills, write them in on your resume. This way, your resume is always up to date.

Have your instructor check your resume when you have finished. This resume can be a valuable tool to serve as a basis for the resume you will write when you actually seek a job.

By going through the steps of writing a resume, you have actually practiced several steps that are helpful in writing essays. You have considered your audience—those who will read your essay. You have organized the information in the most effective manner. After organizing your information effectively, you have presented it in a concise, easy-to-read fashion. All of these steps are also important in essay writing. Now you are ready to choose one or two important areas from your resume to highlight in the cover letter.

Writing the Cover Letter

The cover letter is a business letter that is sent with the resume. It literally "covers" the resume. The purpose of the cover letter is to:

1. Tell the employer what job you are applying for and where you saw the advertisement (paragraph one).
2. Highlight information that shows your qualifications for the position and tell the reader why you are the best person for the job (paragraph two).
3. Tell the employer where he or she may reach you to get additional information or to arrange an interview (paragraph three).

In the cover letter, you must be a good salesperson. The best way to do that is to look at your resume, consider the job you are applying for, and ask yourself what your audience, the employer, will be looking for.

NOW YOU DO IT

Write a cover letter to accompany your resume. Write below one or two things that stand out about you and which you think will help you get the job. These will go in paragraph two of the cover letter.

1. _____
   _____
   _____
   _____

2. _____
   _____
   _____
   _____

Business letters are generally written in block format on 5½″ × 8½″ stationery. They are single spaced and typed on one side of the paper. The upper left-hand corner contains the writer's address (two lines) and the date on a third line. It does not contain the writer's name.

Two lines under the writer's address, type the name and address of the person you are writing to. It should be the same as the name and address on the envelope. Two lines below this address, type the salutation or greeting: *Dear* followed by the person's name and a colon (:). For example, you might write:

Dear Mr. Atkins:

Two lines below the salutation, type the body of your letter. Skip one line between each paragraph. When you are ready to close or end the letter, skip two lines and type:

Sincerely yours,

Notice in the line above that the *S* in *Sincerely* is capitalized but the *y* of *yours* is not. Always place a comma after the closing. Leave four spaces for your signature and type your name.
Look at the sample cover letter that follows and notice the format. This is the standard format for all business letters. Make sure to use the correct business style and format when you write your cover letter.

1435 South Avenue
Orange Park, FL 32073
October 15, 1990

Ms. Charlotte Kaufman
Director, English Language Center
University of Florida
Gainesville, FL 32601

Dear Ms. Kaufman:

I would like to apply for the position of ESOL instructor at the
English Language Center which was advertised in the October 12,
1990, issue of the *Jacksonville Journal.*

I have recently returned to the United States after spending four
years teaching English as a second language at Temple University
in Japan. In Japan, I taught EFL preparatory courses as well as
regular grammar, reading, and writing classes offered at each
level. My experience overseas and my M.A. TESOL from Columbia
University have prepared me well for a position teaching English
as a second language at an American university.

I hope that, after reading the enclosed resume, you will consider
me for the position of ESOL instructor. Please contact me at (904)
264–4467 if you wish additional information or to arrange an
interview. I look forward to having the opportunity to meet with
you to discuss my job qualifications further.

Sincerely,

Richard Anderson

Richard Anderson

enclosure: resume

Writing College Application Essays

Only a year ago many of you were writing college application essays. Yet, you may find that within a short time you will be required to write them again. Some of you may decide to transfer to another college or go on to graduate school, medical school, or law school. If you do, once again you will be faced with having to write another college application essay.

Before you can begin writing a college application essay, you must examine the essay question and think about what it is the admissions people want. Put yourself in their position. As the admissions officer, what would you be looking for?

1. _____

_____

2. _____

_____

3. _____

_____

4. _____

_____

Here are some actual college application essay questions. Read them and determine what information they are seeking.

1. Below is the essay question on the graduate school application, Rochester Institute of Technology, Rochester, NY:

> Please write a statement indicating why you are applying for your pre-ferred program interest, what you hope to achieve through your educa-tion, how it will relate to your long-range career plans, and specifically, why you want to attend this school.

Source: Essay question from the graduate application of the Rochester Institute of Technology, reprinted by permission of the Admissions Office, Rochester Institute of Technology.

Complete the chart analyzing the question on page 36 after you have pre-pared your response to these questions. Remember, the college is also trying to determine how well the applicant can write!

a. What is the *first* thing they want to know?

_____

b. What is the *second* thing they want to know?

_____

_____

c. What is the *third* thing they want to know?

_____

_____

d. What is the *last* thing they want to know?

_____

_____

ANALYZING THE COLLEGE APPLICATION ESSAY QUESTION

INQUIRY	ANSWER (DETAILS, EXAMPLES, REASONS)
I am applying for the ___ program interest because . . .	1. 2. 3.
I hope to achieve ___ through my education . . .	1. 2. 3.
This will relate to my long-range career plan by ___	1. 2. 3.
I want to attend Rochester Institute of Technology because ___	1. 2. 3.

Here is another actual essay question. This one is taken from the undergraduate application at American University in Washington, D.C.:

This personal statement helps us become acquainted with you in ways different from courses, grades, test scores, and other objective data. It enables you to demonstrate your ability to organize thoughts and express yourself. Please write an essay about one of the topics listed below. You may attach extra pages (same size, please) if your essay exceeds the limits of this page.

1. Evaluate a significant experience or achievement that has special meaning to you.

2. Discuss some issue of personal, local, or national concern and its importance to you.

3. Indicate a person who has had significant influence on you, and describe that influence.

Source: Essay question from the undergraduate application of American University, reprinted by permission of the Admissions Office, American University.

NOW YOU DO IT

Which topic would you choose?

What information would you include? Jot down any ideas you have on the topic you chose.

Write the topic and the purpose of the essay on the lines below.

List the ideas you will use to develop this essay.

Next to each idea, write the examples you will use to support each idea.

Topic: _____

Purpose: _____

_____

_____

_____

_____

SAMPLE COLLEGE APPLICATION ESSAY

In response to essay question 1 (Evaluate a significant experience or achievement that has special meaning to you) one student described such an experience in the following essay.

Brette Genzel   1
College Application Essay
December 1987

NOW I CAN DO ANYTHING

I spent eight weeks this summer in Caracas, Venezuela, as an exchange student with Youth for Understanding (YFU). I learned to speak Spanish more fluently, to take chances, and to try new things. As a result, I learned more about myself and the world around me.

One moment I was a sheltered suburban student surrounded by the familiar faces of friends and family; the next moment I was a stranger en route through Atlanta and Miami to Venezuela. My parents would have been proud to see me making the right flight connections, checking my baggage correctly, and dodging people trying to sell me things from books to life insurance.

When the rushing, eating out of tin pans, and lugging of bags stopped, I found myself in a different country looking for a family I had never seen.

During the drive to my new home, I felt like a child discovering snow for the first time. I sat staring out the car window with big bulging eyes, looking at the bright lights on the hills around me. My family was speaking Spanish quickly, and I was trying so hard to understand them that my ears actually hurt.

Once at the house, I dearly clutched my dictionary, looking up almost every word they were saying. I had expected this evening to be awkward but realized we were just five people who happened to speak different languages, and that was all.

The next three weeks I spent shadowing my sister, eating at fast-food restaurants like "Tropi Burger," and fitting in with my new family and friends. I learned Spanish rapidly and soon could communicate without my dictionary!

Unfortunately, I was unaccustomed to the food and for the first few weeks "Pepto Bismol" was my best friend. This did not stop me from trying new things like my Venezuelan mother's favorite dish—cow's stomach, which, incidentally, tastes like a cow smells!

I especially enjoyed hitchhiking into downtown Caracas with my sister to meet friends. We would spend all day shopping, going to movies, or just sitting at a cafe-like restaurant, talking and laughing for hours. It was on these occasions that I picked up the true flavor and spirit of the language and the people.

One weekend I went to Canaima, a jungle in the middle of Venezuela, where Angel Falls—the highest waterfall in the world—is located. For three days I toured throughout the jungle on foot, by jeep, in a canoe, and by plane. I conversed with the native indians and even understood some of their jokes.

My last day in Venezuela, I put myself to the test. Although I was supposed to be picked up from the city by my mother, I decided to make it home on my own. I walked to where I remembered a bus stop and in Spanish asked directions to Cumbres Curumno. The woman answered in Spanish and I understood.

I took three buses and walked several blocks between changes. I picked out the correct change for the bus driver and even had a pleasant chat with a woman from Alto Parado.

That evening I said to myself, "I have really changed. If I could get around a city in a different country where I had just learned to speak the language, then "I can do anything!"

What was her purpose in writing?

What ideas did she use?

What information did she use to support each of these ideas?

Four

Answering Short-Answer Questions

A shocked silence followed after the professor handed out a lengthy midterm test composed of short-answer questions instead of the expected multiple-choice/fill-in-the-blank variety. Finally one student expressed the group's sentiments by grumbling "It's not enough that we have to *know* this stuff. Now we have to *write* about it!"

Short-answer questions are commonly used to test the depth of the student's knowledge and ability to organize and support an idea. To answer these questions effectively, you must:

1. Analyze what the instructor wants to know.
2. Decide on a focus (main point, idea, topic sentence, thesis).
3. Develop examples or supporting documentation to support your idea.

In this chapter, we will develop these skills by using the writing matrix to guide your organization and by using linear development (see page 11, Chapter one.)

The paragraph is the basic unit of all English writing. However, most writing consists of several paragraphs that develop an idea. Nevertheless, there are times when one must respond with a single paragraph. For example, you may have to write a paragraph to answer a question on a short-answer test or write a one paragraph memo.

On the short-answer test, the teacher is often testing your ability to define a term, explain a concept or process, or compare two or more items. How do you respond to a question? One way to respond is to prepare a chart to help you understand the question better and to identify the information the teacher is seeking. As in the college application essay, the first step is to analyze the question.

Analyzing the Question

Let's begin by analyzing each question below to determine what information the instructor wants to know:

QUESTION	INFORMATION NEEDED	TOPIC SENTENCE
1. What is friction?	• What friction is. • How friction works. • An example of friction.	Friction is. . .
2. Give an example of capitalism in American industry.	• What one example of capitalism is.	One example of capitalism in American industry is. . .
3. What new words have computers introduced to the English language?	• List words and show how they are new: byte, trashed, interface, modem.	Many new words have been introduced into the English language because of computers.
4. State two advantages of urban living.	• What two advantages of urban living are. • Examples to illustrate these.	Two advantages of urban living are. . .
5. Contrast oil-based and water-based paints.	How oil-based and water paints are different. Examples to illustrate these differences.	Oil-based and water-based paints differ in their visual characteristics, durability, and ease of cleanup.
6. Explain the difference between intercultural and cross-cultural communication.	What intercultural and cross-cultural communication are. How they are different.	Intercultural communication and cross-cultural communication both deal with understanding culture, but intercultural communication deals with many cultures while cross-cultural communication deals with two cultures only.

NOW YOU DO IT

Analyze these questions and determine the required information. Write a topic sentence for each.

QUESTION	INFORMATION NEEDED	TOPIC SENTENCE
1. Trace the causes of World War II.		

QUESTION	INFORMATION NEEDED	TOPIC SENTENCE
2. Discuss the difficulties that mothers of small children face when they return to work.		
3. What should be done to stop the spread of AIDS?		
4. Explain the advantages of using computers.		

Using the Organizational Matrix

The organizational matrix helps us to develop supporting ideas and guides our writing. Use the organizational matrix in this way:

1. Choose and limit your topic.
2. Decide on *main ideas* to support your topic and list these in the *"Main Idea"* column.
3. Decide upon examples or specific details to illustrate the *main idea*. Place these in the *"Supporting Details"* column.
4. Develop your *topic sentence* by combining your *topic* with your *main ideas*.
5. Use the matrix as a guide to writing your document.
6. Write the conclusion.

Consider this example of an organizational matrix and the resulting paragraph. This paragraph is about individual retirement accounts—special savings accounts designed to provide money for retirement. These accounts are not taxed until the individual withdraws the money when he or she retires.

Question: *What are the advantages of investing in an individual retirement account (IRA)?*

Topic: *Advantages of Investing in an IRA*

Topic Sentence: *An individual retirement account (IRA) is an excellent investment for three reasons.*

MAIN IDEAS	SUPPORTING DETAILS
1. Money and earnings are deferred until retirement.	• Save up to 50% in taxes on each dollar invested during high-income years.
2. Funds can provide supplemental income.	• Supplemental retirement funds and social security income.
3. Money is saved systematically.	• The investor could end up with $1 million from a $60,000 investment.

Resulting Paragraph:

Why would anyone invest $2,000 per year in a bank account he can't draw on until he is 59½? An individual retirement account (IRA) is an excellent investment for three reasons. <u>First,</u> money invested in an IRA is tax-exempt until it is withdrawn. <u>Therefore,</u> one can save up to 50 percent in taxes on each dollar invested during high earning years. <u>Second,</u> IRA funds will provide a welcome supplement to social security and other retirement funds. <u>Third,</u> through the systematic saving of $2,000 per year for 30 years, an individual may receive $1,000,000 for his $60,000 cash investment. This excellent financial return makes the IRA a wise investment for the future.

Using Transitional Words:

In the resulting paragraph, you will notice that certain words are *underlined.* These are called *transitional words* because they allow ideas to flow more freely and make transitions between thoughts. A list of these words and additional discussion of their use is found in the *Reference Section* (Chapter 11). Use them when you develop your paragraphs.

NOW YOU DO IT

Choose one of the questions you analyzed in the previous exercise. Use the *organizational matrix* to develop main ideas and supporting details. Make certain that each main idea relates directly to the topic and that each supporting detail adds concrete information about the main idea.

You may either write your topic sentence first and focus your main ideas on the topic sentence or you may develop your ideas using the matrix and then develop your topic sentence.

After your instructor has checked your work, write a paragraph to support your thesis, using the organizational matrix as a guide.

Question: _____

_____

Topic: _____ _____

**Topic
Sentence:** _____

_____

MAIN IDEAS	SUPPORTING DETAILS

MAIN IDEAS	SUPPORTING DETAILS

Comparison or Contrast Paragraphs

Writing paragraphs for **comparison** or **contrast** questions requires careful analysis. Instead of developing a single set of main ideas and details to support your topic sentence, you must analyze the topic to find common main ideas and then develop specific details for each compared or contrasted item.

Consider the example below. Notice that transitional words are used to emphasize parallel ideas.

Question: *Contrast oil-based and water-based wall paint.*

Topic: *Oil-based vs. water-based wall paint*

Topic Sentence: *Oil-based and water-based wall paint differ in their visual characteristics, durability, and ease of cleanup.*

AREA OF CONTRAST/ COMPARISON	OIL-BASED (ITEM 1)	WATER-BASED (ITEM 2)
VISUAL CHARACTERISTICS	Glossier finish. Richer color.	Matte finish. Less color depth.

AREA OF CONTRAST/ COMPARISON	OIL-BASED (ITEM 1)	WATER-BASED (ITEM 2)
DURABILITY	Can withstand scrubbing. Seldom fades when exposed to bright sunlight over extended time periods.	Loses color or fades through when scrubbed vigorously. Sometimes fades when exposed to bright sunlight over extended time periods.
EASE OF CLEANUP	Requires turpentine to clean brushes. Cannot be washed out of clothes or removed from fabric. Cannot be wiped off easily if spilled.	Brushes can be cleaned with soap and water. Can be washed out of clothes or fabrics when the paint is wet. Can be wiped up with water until dry.

Resulting Paragraph:

Oil-based and water-based wall paints differ in their visual characteristics, durability, and ease of cleanup. In terms of visual characteristics, oil-based paint provides a glossier finish and a richer color than the duller, matte finish of water-based paint. Oil-based paints are also more durable because, unlike water-based paint, they can withstand scrubbing and seldom fade when exposed to bright light over extended time periods. However, water-based paints are easier to cleanup. To remove water-based paints from brushes or clothes, one only needs warm water and soap. Oil-based paints must be removed from brushes with turpentine and cannot be removed from furniture or clothing.

Using Transitional Words:

In the resulting paragraph the underlined words are transitional words. In a comparison and contrast essay, they are used to show the similarities and differences between ideas. See Chapter 11 Reference Section for more information on transitional words.

NOW YOU DO IT

Choose one of the questions below and develop a paragraph using the organizational matrix as a writing guide. After you analyze the question, list comparison/contrast areas in the *areas of contrast/comparison* spaces. Then list supporting details and examples for each item you are comparing/contrasting. For example, if you are developing question 1, item 1 would be nuclear power and item 2 would be fossil fuel power. Usually comparison/contrast development is organized to show that one choice is better than the other.

Questions:

1. To meet increasing energy demands, should countries build nuclear or fossil fuel-powered generation plants?
2. Compare and contrast liberals and conservatives.
3. Compare and contrast American and foreign-made cars.
4. Compare and contrast rock 'n roll of the 50's and the rock 'n roll of the 80's.
5. Choose a comparison and contrast topic of your own.

Topic: _____

Topic Sentence: _____

_____

AREAS OF CONTRAST/ COMPARISON	ITEM 1	ITEM 2

AREAS OF CONTRAST/ COMPARISON	ITEM 1	ITEM 2

After your instructor has checked your work, write your paragraph.

Questions from Subject Areas

LITERATURE

In a literature course, students are often asked to read a poem, novel, or play and then to discuss its elements, theme, or significance. Sometimes students are asked to discuss the plot or character development. Below is a sample question.

Question:

Read the following poem by Robert Frost and analyze its meaning. Use the questions which follow to guide your discussion. Be sure to include some examples of symbolism in your paragraph.

THE ROAD NOT TAKEN

Two roads diverged in a yellow wood,
And sorry I could not travel both
And be one traveler, long I stood
And looked down one as far as I could
To where it bent in the undergrowth;

Then took the other, as just as fair,
And having perhaps the better claim,
Because it was grassy and wanted wear;
Though as for that the passing there
Had worn them really about the same,

And both that morning equally lay
In leaves no step had trodden black.
Oh, I kept the first for another day!
Yet knowing how way leads on to way,
I doubted if I should ever come back.

I shall be telling this with a sigh
Somewhere ages and ages hence:
Two roads diverged in a wood, and I—
I took the one less traveled by,
And that has made all the difference.

Source: Robert Frost, "The Road Not Taken." Copyright 1916 by Holt, Rinehart, and Winston, Inc. and renewed 1944 by Robert Frost. Reprinted from THE POETRY OF ROBERT FROST edited by Edward Connery Lathem, by permission of Henry Holt and Company, Inc.

Here are some questions to guide your thinking:

1. What is the poem about?

   _____

   _____

   _____

2. What could the two paths represent?

   _____

   _____

   _____

3. How are the two paths different?

   _____

   _____

   _____

4. Why did the poet take the one "less traveled by"?

   _____

   _____

   _____

5. Have you ever had to make a difficult decision? When you thought about it, did you choose the path others had taken or did you do something different or untried?

   _____

   _____

   _____

6. How has the poet's choice made "all the difference"?

_____

_____

_____

After you have answered these questions, write a paragraph to answer the question. In your *topic sentence*, be sure to include the name of the poem and the poet as well as what you think Frost is saying.

Topic: _____

**Topic
Sentence:** _____

_____

MAIN IDEAS	SUPPORTING DETAILS

BUSINESS

Sometimes an instructor gives students a table of information and asks them questions about it.

Question:

Examine the table below and write a paragraph to explain which bank and rate you would select to finance your car loan.

AUTO LOANS

Rates shown are the lowest fixed rates available with a 10 percent down payment and the variable rates as of Aug. 13 on a 48-month new-car loan. Some banks may offer different rates for customers and non-customers.

Bank	Fixed	Var.
Anchor Savings	10.15	n.a.
Central Trust Co.	11.05	10.10
Chase Lincoln	10.40	9.20
Chemical Bank	11.90	n.a.
Citibank	11.75	n.a.
Columbia Banking	11.50	10.11
Eastman Savings	10.25	n.a.
Empire of America	11.20	n.a.
First Federal	10.75	9.85
First National	10.50	n.a.
Goldome	10.25	9.25
Key Bank	10.25	10.25
Lyndon Guaranty	10.25	n.a.
Manufact. Hanover	11.40	10.90
Marine Midland	10.95	9.95
Norstar	11.00	10.00
Rochester Community	11.00	9.90
Wyoming County Bank	10.90	na
Credit Unions		
Hilton Federal	9.50	12.00
Penfield	9.90	n.a.
Pittsford	9.75	9.50
Rochester & Monroe Cty. Empl.	n.a.	9.00
Rochester School Empl.	9.75	9.00
Rochester Ukrainian	9.00	n.a.
Summit	10.20	9.00
Webster Federal	8.90	n.a.
Wegmans	9.00	n.a.
WCTA	8.90	9.00

Hints:

Definitions: **VAR.** = Variable interest rate—a rate which can change as the interest rate changes.

FIXED = Fixed rate—a rate of interest that will not change but which requires a 10 percent deposit.

Source: "Auto Loans," *Rochester Democrat and Chronicle,* August 15, 1987. Reprinted by permission of Gannett Rochester Newspapers. *Source of data:* The Winters Group.

After you analyze the table, use the *organizational matrix* to guide your writing. Your *topic sentence* should state your preference and your reason. The supporting sentences should explain your reasoning.

Topic: _____

Topic Sentence: _____

_____

MAIN IDEAS	SUPPORTING DETAILS

FINANCE

Often a professor will give students an article and ask them to analyze and apply their findings.

Question:

Read the following article and study the accompanying graph. Explain why a "bull market" helps individuals. Be sure to use examples to support your argument.

Here are some questions to guide your thinking:

1. What does the professor want to know?

   _____

   _____

   _____

2. What is a bull market? If you don't know, look in a dictionary.

   _____

   _____

   _____

3. Who owns the greatest percentage of stocks? Mutual funds?

   _____

   _____

   _____

4. Who does most of the trading?

   _____

   _____

   _____

5. Where do institutions have most of their money?

   _____

   _____

   _____

6. Where do individuals have most of their money?

   _____

   _____

   _____

7. Why do individuals benefit when institutions do well?

   _____

   _____

   _____

8. According to this article, how do people act when they think they are getting richer?

   _____

   _____

   _____

Action on the market
Odd lots, 1981–1987
In Millions

Stock Mutual Fund sales, 1987
In billions

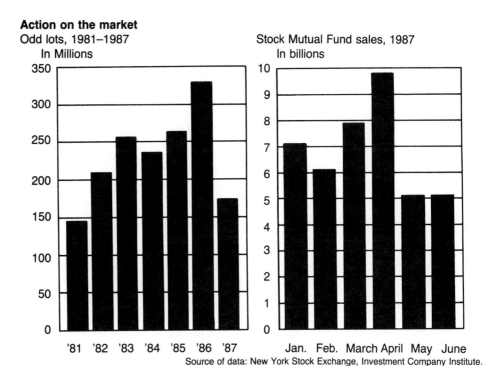

'81 '82 '83 '84 '85 '86 '87   Jan. Feb. March April May June

Source of data: New York Stock Exchange, Investment Company Institute.

HEALTH IS CONTAGIOUS

Bull Market Helps Individuals As Well

By Phil Ebersole and Ed Lopez

The seemingly unkillable bull market celebrated its fifth birthday this week with a strong advance in the Dow Jones Industrial Average.

The Dow finished the week at 2,685.43, setting a weekly advance record of 93.43 points.

The five-year bull market has certainly brought joy to Wall Street, but has it been good for Main Street?

Jeff Schaefer, senior vice president with the Securities Industry Association, said the answer is "yes."

Households, not the so-called institutional investors, own the greatest percentage of stocks, he said.

"People confuse trading with ownership," he said. "Most shares are owned by individuals and most trading is done by institutions."

According to Schaefer, out of a total of $3 trillion worth of equity holdings at the end of 1986, households owned $1.9 trillion compared with $1.1 trillion for institutions.

He also said the percentage of trading by institutions is not as great as is generally assumed.

But Schaefer said institutions may have seen their investments do better than individuals.

That's because the institutions have more of their holdings in blue-chip stocks—which have benefitted most from the market rally—while individuals have more money in secondary stocks.

Statistics from the New York Stock Exchange indicate that small investors have been increasingly participating in the stock market. The volume of odd-lot sales—sales involving less than 100 shares—has grown from 211 million shares from the start of the bull market in 1982 to 329 million shares at the end of 1986.

Several market observers said that when institutional investors do well, individuals benefit from those gains.

That's because it is individuals who are closely linked with such large institutional investors as mutual funds, pension funds, corporate profit-sharing plans, union pension funds, variable annuities and insurance policies.

"A lot of times people say that the market is so institutionally oriented that the individual investor doesn't participate, but that's not the case," said Michael J. Spagnola, vice president and resident manager of Prudential-Bache securities in Rochester.

Spagnola and others noted that

55

many individuals have turned to mutual funds—a major type of institutional investor—as a way to invest in the stock market.

The Investment Company Institute, the trade association for the mutual fund industry, reports that the number of mutual funds has grown from 857 in 1982 to 2,063 at the end of June.

But Lester Thurow, an economist at Massachusetts Institute of Technology, said the five-year runup in stock prices has little significance for ordinary Americans.

Most Americans aren't investors in the stock market, he said, so they gain nothing directly from the bull market.

And while they may depend indirectly on the stock market for retirement income through pension funds, corporate profit-sharing plans, annuities or insurance policies, five years is too short a time to be significant for these forms of investment, he said.

The question is whether gains in stock prices will outrun inflation over 40 years, he said.

A five-year bull market might be canceled out, he said, if it's preceded or followed by a five-year bear market.

Murray Weidenbaum, director of the Center for the Study of American Business at Washington University in St. Louis, said the rising stock market is helping business to make necessary investment.

From 1981 on, he said, business investment in scientific research has exceeded government support of research.

High R&D spending is necessary for American business to compete, Weidenbaum said, and would have been harder to do without the current bull market on Wall Street.

While some companies are investing in new buildings, equipment and research, others are investing in acquisitions of other companies, repurchasing stock from their own stockholders, or borrowing money for leveraged buyouts—buying companies with borrowed money that's paid back by selling assets and siphoning off profits.

Overall, though, Weidenbaum said more is being invested in plant openings and expansions than in plant closings and shifting of operations overseas.

Thurow said companies don't become any richer just because the shares they've already issued are being bought and sold at higher prices.

While rising stock prices do make it easier for companies to issue new stock to finance investment, he said there's little indication they're doing so.

If fact, he said, more companies are buying back their stock than issuing new stock—a fact that itself accounts for part of the rise in stock prices.

Ronald Fielding, manager of five Rochester-based mutual funds, said stock buybacks aren't necessarily a bad thing. If Exxon Corp. spends $10 billion to buy back shares from stockholders rather than using it to search for oil, that indicates that "at the present, we don't need any more oil."

The money doesn't disappear from the economy, he said. The Exxon shareholders may find other and better ways to invest or spend it.

Paul Wachtel, an economics professor at New York University, said a rising stock market also helps the economy by sustaining consumer spending.

Studies show that as long as people think they're getting richer, even if only on paper, they're more ready to buy things, he said.

Thurow said rising stock prices also represent $200 billion in investment by foreigners, who've accumulated dollars as a result of the U.S. foreign trade deficit.

While it's encouraging that foreigners have confidence in the future of the American economy, he said, it means they'll wind up as owners of a bigger fraction of corporate America.

The American nation is, in effect, selling off assets to maintain consumption, he said.

Thurow also said there's less to the bull market than meets the eye. Adjusted for inflation, he said, stock prices have only recently reached 1965 levels and are far short of their all-time highs in the early 1970s.

Source: Phil Ebersole and Ed Lopez, "Health Is Contagious," *Rochester Democrat and Chronicle,* August 15, 1987, p. 70. Published by permission of Gannett Rochester Newspapers.

Use the organizational matrix to guide your writing. Remember that your topic sentence must tell why or how the bull market helps individuals.

Topic: _____

Topic Sentence: _____

_____

MAIN IDEAS	SUPPORTING DETAILS

Your instructor may ask you to write an answer in response to the question.

PSYCHOLOGY

Question:

Read the following article and explain why laughter is beneficial. Write a paragraph supporting your answer. Be sure to use specific examples.

Here are some questions to guide your thinking:

1. What does the instructor want to know?

_____

_____

_____

_____

2. Who is Norman Cousins?

_____

_____

_____

_____

3. What effect does laughter have in the workplace?

_____

_____

_____

_____

4. In what ways is laughter beneficial?

_____

_____

_____

_____

5. What is the effect of humor on children?

_____

_____

_____

_____

6. What conclusion can you come to?

_____

_____

_____

_____

After answering the questions, turn to the organizational matrix that follows the article.

HUMOR FOUND TO AID PROBLEM-SOLVING

Creative Thinking as Well as Social Bonding Are Among Its Benefits, Researchers Say.

By Daniel Goleman

"In America, everything is permitted that's not forbidden," a European joke has it. "In Germany, everything is forbidden that's not permitted. In France, everything is permitted, even if it's forbidden. And in Russia, everything is forbidden, even if it's permitted."

Such jokes suit the notion that much humor veils aggression, permitting the joke-teller, in Freud's words, "to be malicious with dignity." But Freud's longstanding analysis of humor as the release of repressed feelings is receding as a growing group of social scientists, for whom humor is no joke, make it the focus of serious research. In the new work, humor is seen less as disguised hostility and more as a stimulant to problem-solving and productivity, as an aid to education and as the stuff of social bonds.

Humor and its uses have been a subject of conjecture since Aristotle, and a large body of psychoanalytic literature deals with jokes. But "humor has been a neglected topic among researchers," said Donna Cooper, a psychologist at the University of Connecticut who is a consultant on the uses of humor in organizations. "Most psychologists are preoccupied with grim topics and problems. Humor and the positive emotions get little interest or funding."

Of late, though, that has begun to change. Some of the more visible new research, inspired by Norman Cousins' account of how watching Marx Brothers movies and other comedy films helped him recover from a debilitating illness, deals with links between positive feelings and healing.

Less well known is recent research suggesting that putting people in a good mood by telling them jokes makes them think through problems with more ingenuity. Casual joking at work may thus improve people's effectiveness in their tasks.

"Any joke that makes you feel good is likely to help you think more broadly and creatively," said Alice M. Isen, a psychologist at the University of Maryland in Baltimore. The elation that comes from hearing a good joke, Dr. Isen has found, is similar to that which people feel when they receive a small, unexpected gift. Such elation, her research shows, facilitates innovation.

In the research, reported in a recent issue of The Journal of Personality and Social Psychology, Dr. Isen found that people who had just watched a short comedy film of television "bloopers" were better able to find a creative solution to a puzzling problem than were people who had watched a film about math or who had exercised.

The problem posed was one frequently used in such research: People were given a candle, matches and a box of tacks and asked to attach the candle to a corkboard wall so that the candle would burn without dripping wax on the floor.

Most people who try to solve this problem fall prey to "functional fixedness," the tendency to see the objects presented them only in terms of their conventional uses. Those who were in a good mood from watching the funny film, however, were generally able to solve the problem by seeing another use for the box holding the tacks: They tacked the box to the wall and used it as a candleholder.

In other studies, Dr. Isen found that the comedy film increased people's ability to think more broadly, seeing relationships that otherwise eluded them. This is a mental skill that is important in finding creative solutions to problems and in foreseeing the consequences of a given decision. The ability to recognize complex relationships and far-flung implications has also been found, in other research, to mark the most successful business executives.

"The mind associates more broadly when people are feeling good after hearing a joke," said Dr. Isen. "They think of things they ordinarily would not and have access to a broader range of mental material. And the more ideas present in your mind, the more ways you see to connect things; you're able to see more solutions."

BEYOND SATISFACTION

In light of this and other research, joking at work is being appreciated as more than mere diversion. Research to be reported next month at the annual

59

meeting of the American Psychological Association shows that the feeling of having fun at work is more important than overall job satisfaction in workers' effectiveness.

In a survey of 382 people from a wide variety of work places, David Abramis, a psychologist in the School of Business Administration at California State University at Long Beach, found that those who felt their work was fun performed better and got along better with co-workers than did those who were satisfied with their jobs but did not see them as fun.

Traditionally, psychologists have focused on people's sense of satisfaction with their jobs as a measure of their psychological adjustment to work. Dr. Abramis, though, believes that the feeling that one's work is fun is of equal importance and that job satisfaction and having fun at work are independent considerations.

A major source of fun at work, the study showed, is joking with fellow workers, according to Dr. Abramis. "If you are trying to improve people's performance at work, it is not enough to improve their job satisfaction," he said. "Increasing their sense of having a good time at work improves their performance over and above satisfaction."

Joking also has its dangers, particularly carelessness, according to Dr. Isen. "If you want a jocular environment at work, you need to make sure people keep in mind the importance of their work," she said. "If you don't, feeling good may make people sloppy where they should be plodding. But if you tell people who are feeling good that they have made a mistake, they are especially thorough in correcting their errors."

IMPLICATIONS FOR CHILDREN

Although it is a relatively new idea that joking may enhance productivity at work, humor has long been used to make learning more palatable for children, as "Sesame Street" demonstrated. At first, some educators argued that such humor was detrimental to learning, because it drew children's attention away from the serious parts of the material presented. More recently, though, interspersing humor among the serious has been shown to improve children's learning, provided the humor is of the right sort.

New research on which sorts of humor aid learning and which hinder it shows that when the humor distorts the information, it often confuses children. According to findings by Dolf Zillman, a psychologist at Indiana University, irony is particularly confusing to young children, who do not yet have the basic knowledge that would allow them to see what is true and what is a distortion. Dr. Zillman cites as an example of distortion a "Sesame Street" depiction of seat belts on an airplane; when the plane turns upside down the seat-belted characters hang from the cockpit as if the belts were rubber.

Children up to fourth grade, and perhaps beyond, are often confused by such distortions, Dr. Zillman reported in the "Handbook of Humor Research" (Springer-Verlag). On the other hand, he has found that humor that does not distort generally enhances children's ability to master new material. The solution he recommends is to use jokes that are unrelated to the topic at hand, rather than jokes about the information itself.

THE MATURING PROCESS

By the time students reach college age, though, humor that is unrelated to the educational topic can backfire, Dr. Zillman warns. A lecturer who habitually tells such jokes may be viewed as digressing, according to Dr. Zillman, and the joking asides seem to interfere with the students' grasp of the material presented. On the other hand, lecturers who weave into their material humor about the topic seem to be more effective.

Exactly what people find funny changes as they age, according to a survey of 40 stand-up comedians performed by Lucille Nahemow, a psychologist at the University of Connecticut. "Adults of all ages respond to sexual humor," she said, "while younger audiences like aggressive humor, such as put-down jokes, and older audiences like jokes about family life."

Jokes serve an important social function in strengthening the bonds between people, researchers are finding. By laughing at the same things, people let one another know that they have a similar outlook, without having to say so. This makes jokes especially important in communicating about discomforting topics.

"Many jokes are a way to talk about troubling topics like sex and racism," according to Alan Dundes, a folklorist at the University of California at Berkeley, who in "Cracking Jokes" (Ten Speed Press) analyzes the hidden meanings of humor. By laughing at a joke the listener tacitly signals that he shares the attitude implied in it, Dr. Dundes argues.

"Wherever there is anxiety in a culture, you find humor," Dr. Dundes said. "In Eastern Europe, for example, you find many more jokes about politics and Russians than you do in the West, where these concerns are not so overriding."

Indeed, Dr. Dundes takes the popular jokes of a people as a barometer of their hidden concerns. Of particular significance, he finds, are "joke cycles," jokes on a single topic that spring up suddenly, have many variations and are extremely popular. Thus, in his view, "Jewish American princess" jokes of the late 1970's were a reaction to feminism.

"All jokes are serious, and anything funny is at someone's expense," Dr. Dundes said. "It is hard to find a truly harmless joke, one without a serious overtone."

Source: Daniel Goleman, "Humor Found to Aid Problem Solving," *New York Times,* August 4, 1987. Copyright © 1987 by The New York Times Company. Reprinted by permission.

After you answer the questions on "Humor Found to Aid Problem-Solving," use the organizational matrix to guide your writing. Remember that your topic sentence should indicate that laughter on the job is beneficial.

Topic: _____

Topic Sentence: _____

_____

MAIN IDEAS	SUPPORTING DETAILS

MAIN IDEAS	SUPPORTING DETAILS

CHEMISTRY
Writing Up an Experiment

Directions:

1. Assemble the following objects: ground pepper, liquid soap, small bowl filled with water.
2. Sprinkle the pepper on the surface of the water.
3. Place one drop of soap in the center of the dish with the water and pepper.
4. In one paragraph, write how the experiment was conducted and what the results were. If you can explain what happened, you may do so. *Hint:* The explanation has to do with the surface tension of the water.

Use the organizational matrix as a guide for your writing.

Purpose: _____

STEPS OF EXPERIMENT:

RESULT:

EXPLANATION:

Writing a Lab Report

If you have taken science courses, you know that there is a definite format to be used in writing a lab report. While the requirements may vary from teacher to teacher, the following represents the general outline for a lab report.

1. *Purpose or objective.* Like the thesis sentence, which you will study in the next chapter, or the topic sentence in a paragraph, the purpose or objective states the reason for conducting the experiment. (Often it can be stated in one sentence.) Sometimes the reason is simply to find out what will happen.
2. *Procedures.* In this section explain what you did in conducting the experiment.
3. *Data or observations.* This section contains the numbers you have collected from your experiment. It may be in the form of a table or a graph. It may also be a presentation of what you saw when you conducted the experiment.
4. *Results.* This section explains what you have found out from the experiment. Sometimes this section overlaps with the data and observation section.
5. *Discussion or interpretation of results.* This section should reflect on the purpose or objective of the experiment as stated in the first section. It should indicate what you found in relation to the objective or purpose. In some ways this is like the conclusion of an essay. It summarizes what you have said in keeping with your purpose.
6. *Recommendations.* Recommendations are usually required if the project is going to be continued. It may contain suggestions for the project or make recommendations for the future.

Lab Report

Purpose or Objective: _____

_____

_____

_____

Procedures or Experiment: _____

_____

_____

_____

_____

_____

Data or Observations:

_____

_____

_____

_____

Results:

_____

_____

_____

_____

Discussion:

_____

_____

_____

_____

Recommendations:

_____

_____

_____

NOW YOU DO IT

1. In lab report format, rewrite the previous experiment using pepper and water.
2. On a rainy or snowy day, collect some water in a pan. Then with pH

paper, which you can ask a science teacher for, test for the pH of the water. Write up the experiment following the outline for a lab report. (Here is some helpful information: A pH of 7 is neutral, and numbers below 7 are acidic; those above 7 are alkaline. The numbers increase geometrically so that the number 3 is 10 times stronger than the number 4. Numbers from 8 to 14 indicate alkalinity. The value of pure distilled water is considered neutral.) If you continue to do the experiment over a period of time, write up the results to reflect what you have done and what you have discovered. Make a recommendation about acid rain in your vicinity.

3. Drop a stone and a piece of wood into a container of water. The object that sinks has a density greater than water. The object that floats has a density less than water. Water is the standard against which the density of objects is measured. The density of water is 1 gram per milliliter, (g/ml). Write a lab report on this experiment.

4. Follow the same procedure used in number 3 above with other objects of your choosing to find out if their density is greater or less than water. Write up your experiment.

5. If you haven't done the experiment in number 3 above, read the information about density before answering this question. You have two pieces of wood, red maple with a density of 0.75 and greenheart with a density of 1.25. No measuring devices are available and you cannot tell by looking at the wood whether it is red maple or greenheart. Explain how you will determine which piece of wood is red maple and which is greenheart?

Five
Writing the Essay

Question: What nine words do students taking writing courses hate to hear most?

Answer: Write 500 words on a topic of your choice.

Why do students dislike this assignment? They dislike it because it does not narrow the field or provide organizational structure. Unless the student quickly focuses on a specific area, he or she will become bogged down.

Another stumbling block is getting started. Often students can limit the topic and generate main ideas but have difficulty getting the first sentence on paper.

This chapter will help you to:

1. Choose and limit your topic.
2. Generate ideas related to your topic
3. Develop a thesis statement.
4. Learn different essay formats.
5. Write several paragraphs to support an idea.
6. Write an introductory and concluding paragraph.

Writing an essay is nothing more than an expansion of techniques used to write a paragraph. Notice how they compare to each other.

Comparing the Paragraph to the Essay

The Paragraph	The Essay
Attention-getting sentence	Introductory paragraph:
Topic sentence	Attention-getting sentence
	Thesis sentence
	Sentence of method
Body sentences	Body paragraphs:
	Topic sentence
	Support sentences
	Topic sentence
	Support sentences
	Topic sentence
	Support sentences
Concluding sentence	Concluding paragraph:
	Restatement sentences
	Closing sentence

To put this concept in a graphic form, consider the paragraph to be a house. The topic sentence is the foundation, the body sentences are the walls, the concluding sentence is the roof, and the attention-getting sentence is the trim.

An essay, however, can be likened to an apartment building. The foundation is the introductory paragraph, which contains the thesis sentence. Each floor is a topic, which is covered in one or more body paragraphs. The concluding paragraph is the roof. The attention-getting sentence is the trim.

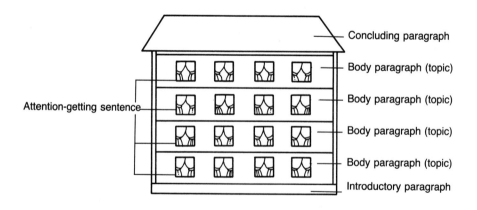

Attention-getting sentence

Concluding paragraph

Body paragraph (topic)

Body paragraph (topic)

Body paragraph (topic)

Body paragraph (topic)

Introductory paragraph

With this in mind, each paragraph in the essay must support the thesis of the essay. Otherwise, the essay will not work. Visually, such an essay would look like this.

It may look funny here, but illogical or careless organization can destroy an otherwise effective document. You can see from the cartoon below what happens when a writer loses focus.

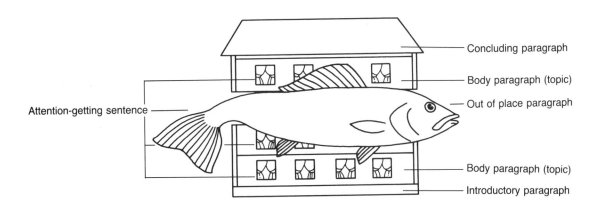

AHEM!

THIS IS MY REPORT ON "HANS BRINKER OR THE SILVER SKATES"

THE MAIN EMPHASIS OF MY REPORT WILL DEAL WITH THE STRANGE SECTION THAT BEGINS ON PAGE SEVENTY-TWO..

Source: Charles Schulz, *Peanuts*. Reprinted by permission of United Feature Syndicate, Inc.

Choosing a Topic

When you are given the freedom to choose your own topic, choose a topic based on the following questions:

1. What do I know a great deal about?
2. What am I interested in researching or learning about?
3. Can this topic be limited (is it limited enough) to fit within the guidelines of the assignment?
4. Is the topic researchable?
5. Will others be interested in the topic?
6. Are there relevant details or examples that I can cite to illustrate the topic?
7. Is the topic appropriate for the course, the assignment, and the reader?

LIMITING THE TOPIC

After you choose your topic, you must limit it to fit the guidelines of the assignment. This will focus your attention and will keep you from wasting effort developing too large a topic.

One excellent way to generate ideas is to use brainstorming. Brainstorming is thinking of all the possibilities and then choosing the ones that best suit the situation.

Consider this example of brainstorming. Here the author is thinking about the things involved in getting a job. The first level of ideas included writing the resume, writing the application letter, and going to the job interview. The second level of ideas included things that were involved in each. This allows the writer to limit the topic.

GETTING A JOB

WRITING A RESUME

WRITING AN APPLICATION LETTER

GOING TO THE JOB INTERVIEW

{ FIRST LEVEL

What it contains

Types of resumes

What the application letter contains

How to prepare for a job interview

Why a good resume is important

Why send an application letter

What interviewers are looking for during a job interview

What to do or not to do during a job interview

{ SECOND LEVEL

Notice that each topic at the second level could be used to develop a 500-word essay. The topics of level one are too large.

Some people, however, like to begin writing on the topic non-stop and see what develops. Then they can go back to the writing and choose ideas that they would like to develop. Others prefer to write lists of words as they occur to them. Then they use this information to guide their essay or as a spring-board to generate ideas.

Let's try an experiment. You must write an essay and the topic of choice is yours. Your mind is a blank. What can you do?

Put your pen to the paper and start writing whatever comes into your head. Keep writing for 10 minutes. If you can't think of anything, write "I can't think of anything." Do not lift your pen from the paper until 10 minutes are up. Now go back and read what you have written. Underline any ideas that emerge which you can use. This is one method people use to generate ideas. Our minds are really never blank!

To try another method, list words, phrases, and ideas that come to mind. Sometimes a word triggers an idea which triggers another idea and so on. Try this for 10 minutes.

Some students draw diagrams. It doesn't matter which method you choose as long as it works for you.

NOW YOU DO IT

Read the following cartoon and two articles dealing with whether English should be the "official" language of the United States. Here are some questions to guide your reading:

1. What is meant by an "official language"?

   _____

   _____

   _____

2. According to Mr. Vazquez, what are the advantages of multilingualism?

   _____

   _____

   _____

3. What trouble did Canada experience when it established both French and English as official languages?

   _____

   _____

   _____

4. According to Mr. Vazquez, what would be the results of declaring English as the official language?

   _____

   _____

   _____

5. According to Mr. Stanwix, why should English be designated as the official language of the United States?

   _____

   _____

   _____

After reading the essays, please answer the questions. Using the brainstorming techniques with a partner, develop a list of five topics relating to the articles which can be covered in 500 words. When you have finished, share your topics with other students in your class.

1. _____
   _____
   _____

2. _____
   _____
   _____

3. _____
   _____
   _____

4. _____
   _____
   _____

5. _____
   _____
   _____

Should English be 'official' tongue?

English!

¡Ingles Y Español!

Source: Bill Mitchell, cartoon, "Should English Be 'Official' Tongue?" *Rochester Democrat and Chronicle*, February 7, 1988. Reprinted by permission.

YES: OUR COMMON LANGUAGE MEANS EQUAL OPPORTUNITY FOR ALL

By John Stanwix

El idioma de Ingles sera el lenguaje oficial de el Condado de Monroe.

Can you read the above statement? My children can't, and they shouldn't be forced to. But they may have to in the future, just to deal with others in day-to-day situations. We as a nation should move swiftly to stem the tide, however well-intentioned, of giving equal legitimacy to a language other than English.

I feel very strongly that English

73

should be the official language of Monroe County and our nation as well. My resolution in the County Legislature, which the Agenda Committee refused to allow to come to a vote before the full body, read simply: "English is the official language of the County of Monroe." My feelings are not jingoistic or ethnically motivated; quite the contrary.

The English language has served as a unifying force in this nation of immigrants for over 200 years. English is historically the language of the United States. English provides equal opportunity for all in the justice system, economics, education, and the workplace.

It is impossible for any government, whether federal, state, or local, to provide services to every individual language population in any jurisdiction.

One group will be discriminated against and another will have special services provided in its native language, just because one language group happens to make up a certain percentage of the population and another does not.

An official English policy will stifle all charges and counter charges of favoritism or discrimination toward individual language groups.

The ever-increasing rise of languages other than English has the potential of tearing at the very fiber that is America.

We need only look across our northern border to observe the boundless complexities caused by rivaling languages in Canada. All national government documents must be printed in both English and French. Furthermore, all national government offices must provide services in both languages. Even the national anthem is sung in French as well as English. I wonder how well the *Star Spangled Banner* translates into Spanish?

Richard Rodriguez, in his autobiography *Hunger of Memory*, tells how, as a young Mexican immigrant with less than 50 words of English he went on to become a Fulbright scholar and earn a doctorate in English Renaissance literature.

"We must be very careful about language," Rodriguez says, "because it's an issue that concerns national stability. Ours is not a bilingual society. We're not Canada or Belgium.

Instead, we're a multilingual society. And unless we accept the imperative of moving all children toward the mastery of English, we risk becoming another Babel."

Rodriguez is not alone in his opinion concerning this issue. *Time* magazine, in its June 13, 1983 issue stated, "A new bilingualism and biculturalism is being promulgated that would deliberately fragment the nation into separate, unassimilated groups . . . The new metaphor is not the melting pot, but the salad bowl, with each element distinct."

And perhaps most disturbing is the revelation by Mayor Maurice Ferre of Miami, who says, "In Miami, you can go throughout your whole life without speaking English at all."

When our European, Asian, and black ancestors came to this country they learned the English language, perhaps not as well as their descendants speak it today, but nonetheless they did learn it. They wanted to become part of America, part of a nation made up of diverse nationalities but joined together by a common language. To some, learning English wasn't merely a practical necessity—it was a moral obligation.

I ask you to support my effort to designate English as the official language of Monroe County. Let's send a message to our state and federal governments that we want to be a melting pot—where all races, creeds, nationalities, and cultures are welcome, accepted for who they are, and joined together.

In the upcoming days, as we reflect on the birth of one of our greatest presidents, Abraham Lincoln, let us recall his words: "A house divided against itself cannot stand."

By the way, the Spanish statement at the beginning of this column reads, "English shall be the official language of Monroe County."

Source: John Stanwix, "Our Common Language Means Equal Opportunity for All," *Rochester Democrat and Chronicle,* February 7, 1988. Reprinted by permission.

NO: THE DIVERSITY OF OUR NATION IS THE SOURCE OF OUR STRENGTH

By Gerardo Vazquez

Every so often the realization comes to me that there are two Americas. One America is bold and moves forward, while the other is frightened and rigid. The question of making English the county's "official" language makes this point painfully clear.

In my view of America we are a pluralistic society with a rich multicultural heritage. Americans and the world celebrate our diversity in race, in ethnicity and in language as the source of our enviable strength as a people.

The other America seems to be a place where there exists a great fear of differences. Fear and intimidation are the responses to natural and positive change.

In the first America multilingualism is a national goal. It is recognized that people who can speak more than one language can help American businesses compete in world markets, and help our nation politically and culturally. In the second America the speaking of another language must be stamped out with ardent reactionary fervor.

In a sad and desperate act functionaries of the California-based U.S. English organization are pressing to officially restrict the use of all languages except English. Monroe County Legislator John Stanwix of Mendon introduced an English-only resolution here.

The proponents of English-only suggest that such laws would promote unity. The opposite is true. In California and Florida the imposition of English-only laws has proven to be very divisive. Bilingual Americans are being harassed by single-language Americans simply for speaking another language.

If Stanwix is interested in language as a unifier, he should witness Pope John Paul II's use of many different languages. The pope is a consummate communicator. Our politicians should be such leaders.

Stanwix cites Canada as an example of bilingualism bringing trouble. What disunity I see in Canada is economically based, and flares occasionally as nationalism in Quebec. There is no comparable situation in this country. Canadians have demonstrated what is the true unifier, and that is respect for people's heritage. To listen to Canadian leaders switch from English to French so fluidly is wonderful.

Stanwix's proposal was vague—it would have made English the "Official" language of the county, but it did not say what that would mean. Imagine the "unity" that could be created: Minority language communities could be deprived of information about health and other concerns from government agencies. They could have been deprived of information they need to vote. Their children could stagnate in classrooms because they could not understand their teachers.

Already in California, proponents of English-only have used a similar state law to file lawsuits against advertising firms, school districts, elections bureaus and even small merchants for having used languages other than English.

Courts could declare non-English speaking defendants guilty because of prohibitions on using interpreters. McDonalds and Pepsi could be banned from advertising in non-official languages. Places of worship might no longer be allowed to use Hebrew, Latin or Hindu.

We Americans of Puerto Rican heritage pose a particularly interesting obstacle to such lunacy. The status of Puerto Ricans both illuminates what America is about and exposes the thoughtlessness of the Stanwix proposal. Puerto Ricans became citizens of the United States decades before Hawaii and Alaska became states. Puerto Ricans are all Americans.

English always will be America's common language. Everybody that I know understands and appreciates that. I've seen the eagerness of people from many countries to learn English, not because it's required, but because it's in their interest. Instead of forbidding the use of other languages, let us deploy sufficient resources so that all Americans who want to learn English have the opportunity to do so.

Last year there was a writing contest for students in bilingual classes here. Read the words of Carmen Sanchez, who was a third-grader at School 17:

My mother does not speak English. When I tell her something in Spanish she tells me to say it in English because she wants to learn the words in English. I am so happy that I know two languages because I can talk to people and play with my friends.

That little girl understands what it is to be an American in a pluralistic America.

The little Carmens of today will be the leaders and voters of 21st-century America. It's their world that we should be building.

Source: Gerardo Vazquez, "No: The Diversity of Our Nation is the Source of Our Strength," *Rochester Democrat and Chronicle*, February 7, 1988. Reprinted by permission.

Developing the Thesis Sentence

The *thesis sentence* is developed from the topic. It is a complete sentence that tells *what you are going to write about.* Examine each of these thesis statements and write what you think the essay will tell about:

1. To prepare for a job interview, you should research the company and be prepared to ask and answer questions intelligently.

   _____

   _____

   _____

2. Interviewers are looking for applicants who meet the job specifications, will fit into the company easily, and are highly motivated.

   _____

   _____

   _____

3. The successful applicant must know dos and don'ts of the job interview.

   _____

   _____

   _____

NOW YOU DO IT

Choose three of the topics you developed in the "Now You Do It" exercise on page 73. Write a thesis sentence for each. When you have finished, ask your partner what he or she thinks your essay would be about.

Topic 1: _____

Thesis Sentence: _____

What the Essay Will Be About: _____

_____

_____

Topic 2: _____

Thesis Sentence: _____

What the Essay Will Be About: _____

_____

_____

Topic 3: _____

Thesis Sentence: _____

What the Essay Will Be About: _____

_____

_____

DEVELOPING IDEAS

The next step is to develop ideas to support your thesis statement. The *organizational matrix* is an excellent tool to help you sort and arrange your ideas. This visual method allows you to see where you need information to support your thesis sentence and to observe the relationships between ideas easily. This creates a framework for your essay and makes it much easier to write. This is a good method particularly if you are a logical thinker or if you need to see how the parts fit together before you tackle the whole.

NOW YOU DO IT

Using the organizational matrix, develop your main ideas and supporting details from either a topic of your choice or from the material you developed in the previous exercise.

Topic: _____

Thesis Sentence: _____

MAIN IDEAS	SUPPORTING DETAILS

The Structure of the Essay

The essay is made up of three important parts: the introduction, the body, and the conclusion.

The *introduction* is a paragraph which introduces the topic and contains the following:

1. An *attention-getting sentence.* This can be a question, a short joke or story, a controversial or emotional statement, or an appropriate quote which relates directly to the thesis sentence. It can also be a series of increasingly specific facts.
2. A *thesis sentence,* which states exactly what the essay will be about.
3. A *sentence of method,* which concisely outlines the main ideas of your essay.

The *body* is made up of two or more paragraphs which explain, defend, illustrate, or inform the reader about the *thesis statement.* Each *body paragraph* should deal with only *one* main idea. Body paragraphs contain the following:

1. A *topic sentence,* which states the *main idea* of the paragraph.
2. *Supporting sentences,* containing supporting reasons, examples, and details to support the topic sentence.
3. *Transitional words or phrases* to make ideas flow.

The *conclusion* is a paragraph which makes a final statement and ties the ideas in your essay together. The conclusion should contain:

1. A *transitional phrase* to signal the conclusion.
2. A brief *restatement* of the thesis and main ideas.
3. A *"closer"* to tie the paper together.

Beginnings and Endings

Interestingly, few students have trouble writing the body paragraphs of their essays. However, they have a great deal of trouble with beginning and ending their essays. Let's discuss writing beginnings and endings.

The introductory and concluding paragraphs are very important parts of the essay. Because the first paragraph often determines whether the reader wants to read the rest of your essay, it has to be interesting and to provide an outline of what the essay will be about.

The concluding paragraph is the last thing the reader sees and remembers. Its purpose is to remind the reader of the thesis and the writer's point of view. It is also the writer's last chance to convince or make an impression on the reader.

Below are introductory and concluding paragraphs that students wrote on the topic of graphoanalysis or handwriting analysis.

INTRODUCTORY PARAGRAPHS

A. Every time we write a letter, an essay, or sign our names, we are letting our reader know a lot more than the literal value of each word. [*attention-getting sentence*] Handwriting gives the reader insight into a writer's personality. [*thesis sentence*] The way a person crosses his "t's" can indicate enthusiasm, stubbornness, or even ambition. Something so simple as dotting an "i" can reveal optimism, dependency, and imagination. [*sentences of method*]

B. The analysis of handwriting has been common for many years. Graphoanalysis, as it is called, was developed by Milton Newman Bunker 50 years ago. [*attention-getting sentence*] Since then, many people have studied and perfected the skill of analyzing handwriting. Many things can be discovered by analyzing a person's handwriting. [*thesis sentence*] I have come to the following conclusions after analyzing the handwriting of Mr. _____. [*sentence of method*]

C. Whoever thought you would be able to tell how aggressive a person may be by analyzing how he crosses his "t's"? [*attention-getting sentence*] Analyzing people's handwriting is a way to unlock the real personality behind the individual. [*thesis sentence*] Follow me now as I try to unveil the personality of my classmate _____ just by analyzing a writing sample. [*sentence of method*]

CONCLUDING PARAGRAPHS

A. In conclusion [*transitional word*], _____ is slightly extroverted and confident. She also seems very well rounded and disciplined. In other words, she knows what she has to do and how to do it. [*restatement*] The findings of this analysis seem to correlate with my impression of _____ from observing her in class. [*closer*]

B. Overall, it can be concluded that [*transitional phrase*] this person is interested in money and people, exhibits emotional control, and can be both private and social. [*restatement*] The broad spectrum of these results points to the low value of this method of assessing people and raises strong questions about the validity of graphology. [*closer*]

NOW YOU DO IT

Examine each of the sample beginning and concluding paragraphs and then answer these questions.

1. Which of the three introductory paragraphs has the most effective attention-getting sentence? Why?

   _____

   _____

2. What do you think the essay will be about for each of the three introductory paragraphs? Why?

   _____

   _____

   _____

   _____

   _____

3. How does the writer intend to prove his or her thesis in each paragraph?

   _____

   _____

   _____

   _____

   _____

   _____

4. Which conclusion is the most effective? Why?

   _____

   _____

   _____

5. Do both writers of the concluding paragraph think that handwriting analysis is a valid way to analyze personality? Why or why not?

   _____

   _____

   _____

   _____

Now that we have discussed the organizational matrix and the paragraphs of the essay, read the following student essay to see how the writer made the transition from the organizational matrix to the essay.

Topic: *How people's characters come out when they do laundry*

Thesis: *As the school year progresses, normal laundry-room patrons become affected by the laundry-room surroundings.*

MAIN IDEAS	SUPPORTING DETAILS
"BACHELORS"	• Don't know how to use a washer or to sort wash (sort by "really dirty, kind of dirty, just worn") • Leads to "gray underwear" syndrome • Leave water and temperature settings as they were • Use soap mysteriously
"MOTHERS"	• Usually those who know how to do laundry • Feel sympathetic and want to help • Bachelors seek them out to do their laundry and supply soap • Are key to the personality of the room
"VULTURES"	• Jump on any available machine without waiting their turn • Take other people's clothes out • Disappear before their "victim" returns to find his or her wet clothes on top of the machine
"REVENGERS"	• Are every vulture's concern • Get revenge on the vulture by tampering with the vulture's washer to keep it from spinning or by throwing lint into the dryer

CHARACTERS OF THE LAUNDRY

Glenn Stott

Approximately once a week, all college students must face the reality of doing their own laundry. [attention-getting sentence] As the school year progresses, these normal laundry-room patrons become affected by the laundry-room surroundings. (thesis statement] These surroundings pressure patrons to take on different personalities. The characteristics of these personalities fall into four categories: the "bachelors," the "mothers," the "vultures," and the "revengers." [sentence of method]

The largest group of laundry-room customers are the bachelors. [topic sentence] They are the group of young men who have never even seen a washing machine, much less done their own laundry. Instead of sorting clothes logically, like "whites," "darks," and "permanent press," they find it more reasonable to sort by "really dirty," "kind of dirty," and "just worn." [supporting sentences]

Bachelors have unique rules for sorting and running washers also. [topic sentence] Another interesting trick of the bachelor is simply not to sort the laundry, but instead just to pack everything into one washer. This procedure usually leads to the "gray underwear" phenomenon. Water-temperature settings follow one basic rule: "Whatever it was set at previously will be just fine." The reasoning behind the amount of soap used per wash remains a mystery. Perhaps it's related to their mood. [supporting sentences]

The mothers of the laundry room are those who know how to do laundry. [topic sentence] Mothers feel sympathetic, if not disgusted, with the young men who wash their wool sweaters in hot water along with their tube socks. Their mother's instinct comes through and they give assistance to these poor misguided students. Of course, the bachelors are well aware this will occur and seek the mothers out. Time after time, they wait to do their laundry until a prospective "bleeding heart" is in the laundry room. With any luck, a smooth-talking bachelor will receive not only advice but also laundry detergent and quarters for the machine. Mothers are, in fact, a definite key to the personality of a laundry room. [supporting sentences]

Vultures are well named. [topic sentence] They sit in the laundry room until some unsuspecting student removes clothing from either the washers or the dryers. Then they jump on the available machine without waiting their turn. Sometimes the vulture throws clothes into the dryer even before the other student has his or her clothes out. Vultures have another dirty trick also. They take other people's laundry out of the machine and stack it on top of the machine so they can use the machine themselves. However, the vultures are never seen. A student will return to remove his or her clothes from the machine, only to discover a pile of wet clothes on top of the washer. No one is around to own up to this action, and even if there was, a vulture would never admit it. [supporting sentences]

The revengers are every vulture's concern. [topic sentence] When a vulture steals a machine, the revengers move in and do their job. If a washer has been emptied of its contents, the revenger's favorite trick is to fix the lid on the vulture's washer so it won't spin. Upon returning, the vulture finds a washer full of soggy clothes instead of spun-dry clothes ready for the dryer. When a vulture empties a dryer, the revengers collect all the lint from the other dryers and throw it in with the vulture's clothes. Therefore, the vulture has a messy surprise waiting for him. [supporting sentences]

In conclusion, all four personalities of the laundry room are crucial to the whole scheme of laundry. [restatement] Not only does this system allow for student interaction, but the analysis of this concept also makes an extremely dull job a little more interesting. [closer]

In addition to noting the function of the sentences, notice how the transitional words, which are the underlined words not enclosed in brackets, connect the ideas and help the flow of information.

NOW YOU DO IT

After your instructor has checked your idea development on page 78, write your essay. When you have finished, exchange your paper with a classmate and discuss the elements of your essay and how you might improve it.

The Process Essay

One of the most challenging papers to write is the *process essay*. The process essay gives directions about how to accomplish a task. Task analysis requires careful attention, because we must decide not only the correct sequence of activities but also the amount of detail to include. Once again, it is important to analyze the audience by answering these questions:

1. What do I want my reader to be able to do when he or she is finished?
2. What must the reader know to accomplish the task?
3. What does my reader know about the topic now? This will give you the amount of detail you must include.
4. What supplies will the reader need to accomplish the task?

To see how this works, let's analyze a simple task: changing a light bulb. The audience will be an individual who has little knowledge of lamps, bulbs, or electricity.

PROCESS ANALYSIS MATRIX

What do I want the reader to do?	Change a light bulb.
What must the reader do to accomplish the task?	1. Unplug and turn off the lamp.
	2. Allow bulb to cool if it was in use before it burned out or remove it using a protective glove or cloth.
	3. Remove the bulb by grasping it lightly and turning it counterclockwise.
	4. Select the correct wattage for the replacement bulb.
	5. Replace the bulb by grasping the replacement bulb firmly but gently and inserting the metal end straight into the socket so that the threads line up. Turn the bulb clockwise until it is seated firmly.

(continued)

What do I want the reader to do?	Change a light bulb.
What must the reader do to accomplish the task	6. Plug in the lamp. 7. Switch on the lamp.
What does the reader know about the topic?	Has little knowledge about lamps, bulbs, or electricity.
What will the reader need to accomplish the task?	Lamp, selection of light bulbs.

CHECKING THE PROCESS MATRIX

After you analyze your task, you must check your information to determine the details you should include. Look carefully at the matrix. Is there any place where you feel a person with little knowledge should have additional information? If you choose "Select the correct wattage for the replacement bulb," you are right. Here is how that section could be improved:

	4. Select the correct wattage for the replacement bulb.
	   a. Bulb wattage determines how much electricity the fixture will use and how much light the bulb will produce.
	   b. Bulbs are usually either 25, 60, 75, or 100 watts. Three-way bulbs—bulbs designed to provide low-, medium-, and high-intensity light—are usually 150 watts but should only be used in lamps designed with a three-way switch.
	   c. Check the light fixture's base plate for maximum bulb size. (Using a bulb with too high a wattage can cause the fixture to overheat.)

WRITING THE PROCESS ESSAY

After developing and checking the *process analysis matrix*, the next step is to use the matrix to develop the process essay. First, develop the *thesis statement*, a sentence which tells what the essay will be about. Second, examine the matrix to develop the *sentence of method*. This is a sentence that gives an overview of the main ideas of the essay. Third, break the material into paragraphs and make certain each has a *topic sentence*, which defines the content of the paragraph. This can be done either by examining the *process analysis matrix* or by transferring the information to an *essay organizational matrix* like the one you completed on page 78.

The essay is completed by writing the *concluding* paragraph, which restates the thesis statement and closes the essay. The *attention-getting sentence* can be written either after the essay is completed or when you first start writing.

Read the following essay and see how the writer uses the *process analysis matrix* to construct her essay.

LET THERE BE LIGHT

"Who turned out the lights!" is a common cry when the light bulb burns out. [attention-getting sentence] Rather than sitting in the dark, you can replace the bulb quickly and easily. [thesis sentence] By taking commonsense safety precautions, making the correct bulb selection, and having a little manual dexterity, you will have the job done in no time. [sentence of method]

The first step is to remove the bulb. [topic sentence] Unplug and turn off the lamp to avoid an electrical shock. If the lamp was in use, allow the bulb to cool off or use a protective cloth or glove to remove it. Otherwise, you may burn your fingers on the hot bulb. Then, remove the bulb by grasping it gently but firmly and turning it counterclockwise until it comes out of the socket. [body sentences]

The second step is to select the correct wattage for the replacement bulb. [topic sentence] Bulb wattage determines how much electricity the fixture will use and how much light the bulb will produce. Bulbs for household use are usually either 25, 60, 75, or 100 watts. Low-wattage bulbs like 25s and 60s are used for soft light, and higher-wattage bulbs, 75s and 100s, are used for reading or high light-demand areas. Three-way bulbs, designed to produce low, medium, and high intensity light, are usually 150 watts but should only be used in lamps designed with a three-way switch. However, one should check the light fixture base plate to determine maximum bulb size or circuit load. Using bulbs too high in wattage can overheat the fixture and create circuit overloads or fires. [body sentences]

The last step is to replace the bulb and turn on the fixture. [topic sentence] Replace the bulb by grasping it firmly but gently and lining up the metal core of the bulb straight into the socket so that the threads match. Then with a clockwise motion screw the bulb until it is firmly seated. Finally, plug in the lamp and then switch on the light. [body sentences]

In conclusion, [transitional phrase] changing a light bulb is a simple but gratifying operation. [restatement] By following simple steps and being aware of safety, you will have light in your life once again. [closer]

Notice that the transitional words are used to establish a time sequence.

NOW YOU DO IT

Choose a task that someone could do in the classroom and write a process essay. You may choose one of the topics you did not develop on page 73 giving directions or another of your choice. Use the *process analysis matrix* below to analyze your task and as a guide for your writing. Review your matrix carefully to make sure you have included all necessary information. Have your instructor check your matrix before you write your essay. When you have finished, your instructor will ask you to bring in the necessary materials and have another student follow your directions.

PROCESS ANALYSIS MATRIX

What do I want the reader to do?	
What must the reader do to accomplish the task?	
What does the reader know about the topic?	
What will the reader need to accomplish the task?	

Six

Writing the Narrative

Think back to your childhood for a minute. Remember the stories, some happy, some sad, that your parents or grandparents told you about their lives. Through these narratives, we learned the history of our families, how things were in "the good old days," and how our families viewed the world. I can still remember the colorful stories my father told about his life as a young man in rural Tennessee: how he floated across the wild Tennessee River holding on to a watermelon or how he and his teenage friends reassembled a farmer's wagon on top of his barn on Halloween night.

Take a moment to recall two of your favorite stories told to you by a family member and list them below:

1. _____
   _____

2. _____
   _____

Narratives are the glue that bind generations together. They become the record of our experiences and the log of our dreams.

Narrative writing is one of the most challenging but most rewarding types of writing. However, as in other types of writing, you must choose and limit your topic and organize your material carefully. The development of the narrative can be done in eight steps.

Before we discuss these steps, read the article "Against All Odds" on page 90. We will use this article to illustrate the process of narrative writing.

AGAINST ALL ODDS

Not Everyone Who Goes to College Can be Called a Pioneer

By Martha Graves Cummings

August was so hot the covers of the old textbooks were sticky as I unpacked them. It was 1978, and the school year at Brockport State's Educational Opportunity Center was about to begin.

I had just started to set up my grade books when Jesse, our EOC security guard, strode purposefully into my classroom.

"Well, Doc, looks like you're gonna have a handicapped student in your GED class this semester. Since she uses a wheelchair, we gotta know where she is every minute so's we can evacuate her in case of an emergency," said Jesse, looking very serious.

He said that her name was Frances Agnello and that she had spina bifida.

"That means she was born with an open spine and she's paralyzed from the waist down. Sometimes she can get around on crutches though," he said.

"Does she need special books or help getting around?" I asked.

"Naw, from what I gather, she can do everything herself, but she's gonna have a helluva time getting up the steps into the building or onto the elevator. I don't reckon we're gonna change anything because nobody thinks that she'll last that long around here."

"Have you talked with her yet?"

"Yeah, I met her yesterday. She seems like a nice, quiet, shy kid. And white, yet. She's gonna have a tough row to hoe around here, all right. Hope she gets along ok," Jesse said shaking his head.

I knew what he meant. The Rochester EOC was made up, for the most part, of streetwise, outspoken black adult students who had dropped out of school; some had been to reform school. They were eager to learn, but didn't take anything from anybody. They were, however, fair. They accepted people for what they were or did rather than what they had or said they'd do.

When Fran was wheeled into my classroom, I got the first shock of many. She was no "kid" but a woman who, I was amazed to discover, was 43.

The most striking things about her were her massive shoulders and arms, developed through years of using crutches, and her soft brown eyes, which would not meet mine. Her delicate strawberry blond hair was curled and sprayed exactingly in place. Her tiny hands twisted on one another as she gripped her handkerchief and attempted to control the quiver of her chin. She was no bigger than a 10-year-old and was attempting to make herself even smaller and more insignificant in the raucous classroom.

On the first day of class, students introduced themselves, some telling of their experiences, others of their dreams. Frannie, when her turn came, said nothing. People looked away in deference to her shyness and then someone said, "Come on, speak up. We want to know about you, too, seeing's you know all about us."

Fran hesitated and then, so quietly that the class had to bend forward to hear, said, "I've come to learn . . . just to learn."

Fran worked conscientiously on her lessons and struggled to keep up. Her susceptibility to kidney infections and respiratory infections made her miss crucial classes, but she never gave up or asked for special privileges. She was a fighter and, although she didn't know it, others in the class recognized that and respected her. She always stayed apart from the other students and was painfully shy when someone asked her a question or tried to start a conversation.

A field trip made Fran a part of the group. On a snowy, blustery day in November, our class was slated to take a walking field trip to the Archives Room of the Rundell Library. Usually we took advantage of the free downtown bus service to cover the half mile, but we realized immediately that Fran couldn't take public transportation because of her wheelchair. Mortified that she was a burden on the class, she whispered, "That's ok. You go. I'll just stay here and study."

The rest of the students turned away and began to talk in conspiratorial whispers. Arriving at a decision, they said, "Well, if she can't ride the bus, we'll all walk it together. Take it or leave it!"

"I can't let you do that. It's snowing and cold. You'll freeze to death. After all, I've never been on a field trip before," she said.

"Let us, hell!" exclaimed Dee, the class leader. "What's wrong with you, girl? We're doing what we want to do because we want you along, understand? The only difference between you and us is that you sit around more than we do."

I pushed her in her wheelchair through the snow and up the middle of South Avenue, the busiest street in Rochester, against the traffic. The sidewalks hadn't been cleared. I almost spilled her out three times, but we laughed all the way. Cars splashed us with slush, motorists honked and shouted, and pedestrians gave us odd looks. We didn't care. To us, it was spring.

After this, Fran became involved in social activities at EOC and went on to become a board member of a disabled citizens group. She worked to increase public awareness of the needs and feelings of the disabled. She crusaded to have the city of Rochester make streets and buildings accessible. Even EOC finally recognized that she was there to stay when they created a curb ramp, special restroom facilities, and accessible elevator controls for her and other disabled students who would come after her. She once told me, "All we want is to be treated like everyone else. We want to be seen not as disabled people but as people who happen to have a disability."

Fran learned a lot that year: how to get along, how to assert herself, and how to have a good time. She even learned how to dance in her wheelchair. At the Christmas dance, EOC had a disc jockey who played current hits. As Fran was watching the others glide around the floor, she sighed, "Gee, I wish I could do that."

"Why not," I said, "I'll dance with you."

"What the heck," she exclaimed. "At least I don't have to worry about you stepping on my feet!"

So, even though we were women and one of us happened to be in a wheelchair, we danced to the BeeGees as I held her hand and moved her around the floor. Peter Otero, our EOC counselor, stepped forward to claim the next dance. For the rest of the evening and at every dance from then on, Fran "got down" and boogied with the rest of them.

Frannie worked harder and longer than any other student to achieve her goals and when she succeeded at my level, she passed to the next. At the end of the year, the faculty of EOC elected her "Outstanding Scholar" and she was honored with other outstanding college students at a formal convocation at Brockport State.

As family and friends looked on, the outstanding scholars proceeded into the hall, followed by faculty members. As the students went up to receive their awards, faculty members elbowed each other and sang the praises of their scholars.

When Frannie's turn came, a hush fell over the audience. With dignity, she rose from her wheelchair and laboriously made her way across the stage to receive her award from the college president. Roaring with applause, onlookers rose to give her a standing ovation. A little more enthusiastically than I meant to, I elbowed the black-robed colleague on my left and, glowing with pride, exclaimed, "She's my student. A real winner, huh?" He rubbed his side and grinned back.

However, she didn't always win out scholastically. Even after four tries, she couldn't pass the High School Equivalency Test. The test, which is five hours long, was beyond Fran's fragile strength and endurance. She did come close to passing. But for her, almost wasn't enough. Without a high-school diploma, she could never be accepted to college and become a psychologist.

Finally, however, we hit upon a solution. Monroe Community College of Rochester had a program that allowed students to enter and receive a high-school diploma if they successfully completed 24 hours of college credit. Fran leaped at the opportunity. We worked out a comprehensive plan for her to take two courses at a time and have adequate transportation and support services. She hoped eventually to learn to drive a car with special hand controls, and as her final leap to self-reliance, she hoped to get into a four-year school and move into student housing.

During that year, we became close friends, not just student and teacher. We planned, dreamed, and prepared for the future. We shopped, went to

91

movies, ate out, and explored the city together. I built up muscles lifting her and her wheelchair and she developed laugh lines lifting my spirits. I was her first real friend and during that time together, we shared everything.

As our friendship grew, Fran told me of her lonely childhood and the painful operations she had undergone to correct kidney, bladder, and spinal problems. Her adoring parents, especially her father, tried to shield her from the world and the pain of learning that she was "different." She only got as far as the third grade before she was taken out of school. While she stayed at home, she watched her two sisters go to parties, have dates, go to dances, marry and have children, experiences Fran badly wanted. Although she was the oldest, she often was treated as the "baby" and allowed little choice about her life or education.

Fran's crisis occurred when her father died and she became her mother's main source of emotional support. Suddenly, at 43, she realized that if she were ever to have a life of her own or achieve her dreams of love and independence, she had to begin then.

Coming to EOC was the first step on the road and one that she took without the complete support of her family. Fran once said that her family attempted to shelter her, to limit her independence, not because they were afraid she'd fail but because they were afraid she'd succeed. They loved her so much they didn't want to lose her. She understood. Maybe that's why things happened the way they did.

In August 1979, I left Rochester to take a job in Fort Worth, Texas, knowing that Frannie had been accepted to Monroe Community College. We corresponded back and forth for a while but finally lost track of each other.

When I moved back to Rochester, I meant to locate her but somehow never did until one dark December day when I saw her name in the obituary column. I couldn't believe it: Frances Agnello dead. It had to be another Frances Agnello. She was so young. Then suddenly I realized for the first time she was nine years older than I. Like all the others, I had thought of myself as the older one.

Unwilling to accept her death, I went to the funeral home. All I remember was the coldness and vastness of the room and Frannie in her casket, spotlighted and surrounded by flowers. Dressed in a delicate lace frock, she looked so straight and still. I had forgotten how small she was.

When I spoke to her mother, I discovered Frannie had to drop out of college because of her health and because the family thought it was for the best. She had lived her last year in isolation because she was not well enough to go to social events or to attend her committee meetings. Finally her mother hugged me and said through her tears, "She loved you so much. You two always had such good times together."

I couldn't listen anymore. I hugged her mother and sister and turned back to Frannie. Tears of regret and loss cascaded down my cheeks as I held her hand. I patted her arm and whispered for the last time, "See you around, kid."

And I do. Every time I walk down South Avenue in the snow toward the library.

Steps to Narrative Writing

STEP 1: CHOOSE AND LIMIT YOUR TOPIC

To decide what you want to write about, think about interesting experiences you've had. When you choose an experience, make sure that:

1. You can tell the story in 750 words or less.
2. You will feel comfortable sharing the story with others.
3. The story will be interesting to people in the class.
4. The story has a definite beginning, middle, and end.
5. The story can be told from your point of view (in the first person).

If you have trouble deciding on a topic, discuss possible topics or stories with your friends, family, or people in your class. Often others can suggest things you can write about.

List three possible narrative topics:

1. _____

_____

2. _____

_____

3. _____

_____

Now evaluate each topic using the criteria above. Discuss each with your partner and then decide which topic you wish to develop. Put a star (*) by that topic.

STEP 2: DECIDE ON THE PURPOSE OF YOUR WRITING

The *purpose* is what you want to accomplish with your writing. In "Against All Odds," what do you think the writer wants the reader to know or to understand?

_____

_____

In the space below, write your purpose for writing:

_____

_____

_____

_____

STEP 3: DEVELOP A "STORY LINE" OR PLOT

The story line or plot details *exactly* what you will write about. The best way to develop the story line is to list what happens in your story from beginning to end.

With a partner, list on a separate sheet of paper the events that happen in "Against All Odds," in the order that they are presented in the story. You will notice that details of Fran's early life are added to the story *after* the actual action of the story begins.

Take some time to think before you write. Then list each step of your narrative as it happened from beginning to end. Number each step.

STEP 4: DECIDE HOW MUCH INFORMATION YOU NEED TO INCLUDE IN YOUR NARRATIVE

Adding Important Details

Think carefully to decide how much information the reader needs in order to understand the story. For example, in "Against All Odds," the writer tells the reader in the beginning of the story what spina bifida is and how this affects people who have it.

Why is this important to the reader's understanding of the story?

_____

_____

What are two other important things that the reader learns in the beginning of "Against All Odds"? Why is this information important?

1. _____

_____

2. _____

_____

Now examine your list and add any information the reader will need to understand the story. Write these items in the space below.

_____

_____

_____

_____

_____

_____

Eliminating Unnecessary Information

One of the most common problems in narrative writing is the tendency to include unnecessary or distracting information. For example, in "Against All Odds," the reader learns little about the writer's life because the focus of the story is on Frances Agnello.

Look carefully at your list and eliminate any items which do not relate *directly* to your story. Cross them off the list you developed in Step 3.

STEP 5: DECIDE WHERE YOU WANT YOUR NARRATIVE TO START

A narrative can start anywhere in the action. It can start at the beginning and relate the events chronologically. It can begin at the end and tell the events as a "flashback" or memory. It even can begin in the middle of the action, as in "Against All Odds." The writer begins the story just before she meets Frances Agnello and introduces important background information about Fran's physical condition, people's perceptions of her, and the nature of the students at EOC.

Now decide where you want to start your narrative. List that point in the space below. Then list the information that the reader needs to know to pick up the narrative where you want to begin:

Starting Point: _____

_____

Information the Reader Needs to Know: _____

_____

_____

_____

_____

_____

STEP 6: USE FIRST-PERSON ("I") NARRATION

When you write your narrative, tell your story in first person—I—from *your point of view*. First-person narration is very exciting and effective because it allows you to tell the story as you experienced it. However, you can only include what you would see, know, or be aware of through other people or through your own observation. You cannot see into anyone's mind, know the future, be in more than one place at a time, or know the past other than what you see, are told, or read about.

STEP 7: USE DIALOGUE AND DESCRIPTION TO CREATE A MENTAL PICTURE FOR THE READER

Using Description

Description provides the reader with a mental picture of events. For description to work, it should appeal to as many senses as possible and use words which convey a vivid image. Use your *thesaurus* to find strong, creative words to replace burned out words like "pretty," "good," "bad," "big," "little," or "cute."

Compare the two descriptions of Frannie that occur in paragraphs 9 and 11.

1. How does Jesse describe Frannie in paragraph 9? What does this tell you about how he and the administration perceive her?

_____

_____

_____

2. How does the writer describe Frannie in paragraph 11?

_____

_____

_____

_____

3. How are these descriptions different? Why are these differences in perception important?

_____

_____

_____

_____

Now look over your story-line list and mark the places where you need to add description. List words you will use to describe the person, action, place, or event in the spaces below:

_____

_____

_____

_____

_____

_____

_____

_____

_____

_____

_____

_____

_____

_____

_____

_____

_____

_____

_____

_____

_____

Using Dialogue

Dialogue is the heart of the narrative. _Dialogue_ provides insight into people's perceptions, introduces important information into the narrative, and creates interest and excitement. For example, we learn about Fran's disability and how the EOC administration and staff view her in a dialogue between the writer and Jesse. Using dialogue not only creates a visual picture but saves many paragraphs of description that would have been necessary without this dialogue.

There are some important rules for using dialogue, however. First, listen to people to see how they _really talk._ People seldom use complete sentences or long descriptions except in very formal situations. Make your dialogue sound natural by using incomplete sentences, abbreviations, and slang when appropriate.

Consider the difference between these two lines of dialogue:

1. "Naw, from what I gather, she can do everything herself, but she's gonna have a helluva time getting up the steps into the building or onto the elevator. I don't reckon we're gonna change anything because nobody thinks she'll last that long around here." (paragraph 7)
2. "No, I think she can do everything for herself. She is going to have a great deal of trouble, however, mounting the steps or entering the elevator. I do not think we are going to make alterations in the building because she probably will not be going to school here very long." (revised)
   a. How are these two pieces of dialogue different in word choice and sentence structure?

   _____

   _____

   _____

   _____

   _____

   _____

   b. How does wording influence our perception of Jesse?

   _____

   _____

   _____

   _____

   _____

   _____

c. Which do you prefer? Why?

_____

_____

_____

_____

_____

_____

Here are some other important rules for writing dialogue:

1. Indent and begin a new paragraph each time a different person speaks during a dialogue.
2. Put quotation marks around what an individual actually says.
3. Do not use quotes around "said that" phrases. This is indirect quoting.
4. Put end punctuation inside quotes.
5. Use a phrase like "he said" to indicate who is speaking.

Examples:

(rule 1) He said her name was Frances Agnello and _that_ (rule 3) she had spina bifida.

(rules 1 and 2) "That means she was born with an open spine and she's paralyzed from the waist down. She can get along on crutches though," (rule 2) _he said._ (rule 5)

(rule 1) "Does she need special books or help getting around?" (rule 4) _I asked._ (rule 5)

Now look over your story line and mark places where you want to use dialogue. Write these sections of dialogue in the space below.

_____

_____

_____

_____

_____

_____

_____

_____

_____

NOW YOU DO IT

After your instructor has checked your work, write your narrative. When you have finished, check it to make sure it flows well, contains strong description and dialogue, and is mechanically correct. Ask your partner to read and evaluate your narrative. Consider his or her suggestions and then revise your narrative before you share it with your class or hand it in to your instructor.

Seven

Writing the Persuasive Essay

Hundreds of types of domestic and foreign cars are sold in the United States. However, many are not able to capture a large enough share of the consumer market to be successful. How does advertising make the difference between the success and the failure of a product?

What are some of the ways that advertisers persuade you to buy their car? Choose one car model and state the reasons why you would purchase it. Give as much specific information as you can.

Car Model: _____

Reason: _____

_____

Reason: _____

_____

Reason: _____

_____

When you have finished, share this information with a partner. Would he or she like to buy the car after reading your reasons? Why or why not? What car did your partner choose and why?

Elements of Persuasion

Persuasion can be defined as using reasoning or emotional appeals to convince someone to do something or to believe something.

EMOTIONAL APPEALS

Let's consider emotional appeals first. Some of the most powerful emotional appeals are:

1. To be sexually or physically attractive or desirable.
2. To be powerful or be seen as influential.
3. To "get ahead" or better your position socially or financially.
4. To return to the "old ways" or to reexperience the pleasant things of childhood.
5. To be regarded as an intellectually superior individual.
6. To be the first to do something or to be able to do things others cannot.
7. To escape from reality or from unpleasant situations.
8. To experience or achieve peace or tranquillity.

NOW YOU DO IT

Let's examine how advertisements use these appeals. Choose one magazine advertisement which uses emotional appeals and paste it in the space on page 103. In the space below, evaluate the advertisement.

1. List the emotional appeals and details that the advertisement uses to illustrate them.

   _____

   _____

   _____

   _____

   _____

   _____

   _____

   _____

   _____

2. Is the advertisement effective? Why or why not?

   _____

   _____

   _____

   _____

3. Ask your partner to evaluate the advertisement. Does he or she feel the advertisement is effective? Why or why not?

   _____

   _____

   _____

   _____

Paste your advertisement here:

APPEALS TO REASON

Many times, however, emotional appeals are not enough to persuade the reader to believe or to take a particular action. The most common *logical methods* are:

- ☐ Citing empirical facts
- ☐ Basing judgments on concrete, specific evidence or information
- ☐ Logical analysis of facts, reasons, and examples

To see how this works, let's return to the exercise on page 101 about the automobile. Just because a car is powerful or attractive is not enough to convince most people to purchase it. The consumer wants to know *logical* reasons and *specific information* about why one car is a "better buy" than another. Some of these reasons would include:

1. Durability: How well the car will hold up under adverse road conditions; how long the car body and components will last.
2. Warranty: What the warranty covers, how long the warranty lasts, what conditions would void the warranty.
3. Mileage: How many miles to the gallon the car gets for highway and city driving.
4. Reliability: The car's repair record, how the car behaves in cold or adverse weather.
5. Options: What options come "standard" with the car, what other options are available and how much they cost.
6. Service: Who can fix the car if it has problems, how prices for parts compare with those for other cars, how much it costs to "tune up" the car, whether the dealer or a garage is eligible to do "warranty work."

Can you think of any others?

_____

_____

_____

NOW YOU DO IT

Now that we have analyzed the logical and emotional appeals used by advertisers, it's your turn to write an advertisement. Choose a product or service you are familiar with. Try to find a photograph from a magazine to illustrate your advertisement. Then analyze the product and write an advertisement that will appeal to your buyer. When you have finished, share your advertisement with the class.

Product: _____

Logical Reasons to Purchase It:

_____

_____

_____

_____

_____

Emotional Appeals:

_____

_____

_____

_____

_____

Example of a Persuasive Essay

Like advertisments, persuasive essays require careful planning and organization. You must decide on your thesis, provide specific supporting reasons and examples, and decide on the appeals to convince your reader to agree with you.

Read the student essay "Performance-based Learning." Then answer the questions on page 107.

PERFORMANCE-BASED LEARNING

Mary Smallwood

Students are obsessed with grades, not learning. Why else would they put in "all nighters" to memorize data they'll forget immediately or devise elaborate schemes to cheat on exams? Rather than a system that places a point value on learning and forces students to compete against each other, American universities should use a performance-based system which measures individual performance against a set standard.

In the traditional system, students compete against each other rather than against a set standard. Many college tests are "curved" so that 5% of students receive "A's" or "F's," 15% receive "B's" or "D's," and 60% receive "C's." For example, if the average grade on a 100-point test is 90, a student who receives less than 82 points would fail. By the same token, 90 points would equal a "C." This arbitrary standard creates wide variations in the "value" of a grade and the assessment of student achievement.

Often, however, grades in the traditional system are derived by a point system. In many colleges, 92–100 is an "A," 85–92 a "B," 75–84 a "C," 65–74 a "D," below an "F." However, these numbers, since there is no standard or condition for performance, mean little. For example, if a student scores 75% on a pharmacy final, does this mean he can dispense only 75% of the required prescriptions? What will happen when he must use the 25% he doesn't know?

Performance-based instruction is based, not upon an arbitrary standard, but upon a standard and conditions required to do a task effectively. From the beginning, the students know exactly what they are expected to learn, how they will be tested, and the level of performance they must achieve. There are no percentages or grades. Either a student can or cannot do a task. These objectives create the structure for learning and serve as a study guide for the learner.

Performance-based objectives contain an action the student is to do, the condition he is doing the action under, and the required level of performance. The following is an example of a performance-based objective:

Upon completion of this lesson (condition), the student will be able to determine the concentration of flouride ions in a sample and interpret and record the results of the analysis (action) without error (performance level).

The student passes the test only if he can perform the task without error. He competes against himself rather than with others.

In conclusion, changing to a performance-based system would require a major shift in traditional instructional and testing methods. However, a performance-based system would ensure that "passing" a course results from acquiring specific knowledge and skills rather than achieving an arbitrary percentage on a test.

Questions:

1. What is the writer's thesis?

_____

_____

2. What is the effect of the first and second sentences of the essay?

_____

_____

3. How are test grades derived in the traditional American system?

_____

_____

4. Why does the writer say this is a less than effective method?

_____

_____

5. What is performance-based learning?

_____

_____

6. What are the advantages?

_____

_____

7. Do you agree with the writer? Why or why not?

_____

_____

8. What kind of grading system do other schools you have attended use?

_____

_____

_____

NOW YOU DO IT

1. Reread the two persuasive essays on whether English should be the official language in the United States. Prepare the organizational matrix on

pages 108–109 for each essay. With your class, discuss what means of persuasion each writer uses.

2. With your class, brainstorm a number of questions that have two sides. Here are some examples:

   a. Which is the better fuel for electrical generation: fossil or nuclear fuel?
   b. Should people be allowed to smoke cigarettes in restaurants or other public places?
   c. Should unmarried students be allowed to live together in university housing?
   d. Should freshmen be required to live on campus their first year?
   e. Should there be a minimum wage?

After you have chosen a topic, use the organizational matrix to organize your material and to guide the writing of your essay. When you have finished, share your essay with your partner.

ORGANIZATIONAL MATRIX/ENGLISH SHOULD BE THE OFFICIAL LANGUAGE: YES!

REASONS	SUPPORTING DETAILS/EXAMPLES

ORGANIZATIONAL MATRIX/ENGLISH SHOULD BE THE OFFICIAL LANGUAGE: YES!

REASONS	SUPPORTING DETAILS/EXAMPLES

ORGANIZATIONAL MATRIX/ENGLISH SHOULD BE THE OFFICIAL LANGUAGE: NO!

REASONS	SUPPORTING DETAILS/EXAMPLES

109

ORGANIZATIONAL MATRIX/ENGLISH SHOULD BE THE OFFICIAL LANGUAGE: NO!

REASONS	SUPPORTING DETAILS/EXAMPLES

Use this matrix to develop your ideas in response to one of the questions on page 107.

ORGANIZATIONAL MATRIX:

REASONS	SUPPORTING DETAILS/EXAMPLES

ORGANIZATIONAL MATRIX: _____

REASONS	SUPPORTING DETAILS/EXAMPLES

Eight

Taking Notes for the Research Paper

Question: Besides final examinations, what one item are course grades most often based on?

Answer: A research paper.

No wonder research papers are so important! During a college career, the average college student will write twelve research papers. Doesn't it make sense to learn to do the job well?

Let's begin by defining what we mean by "research paper." A research paper is a composition based on information gathered from a variety of sources. That means, instead of writing a composition based on your experiences and opinions, you investigate the information available on the subject and use this information to illustrate or support your main idea. In some ways, the research paper you write is a contribution to your field and represents the data available on the subject.

Needless to say, the most important part of the research paper is the content—the information you present. To write a well-documented paper, you must understand the rules of documentation and methods of taking notes. That's what you will learn to do in this chapter.

Plagiarism

Although the research paper is often the most challenging and interesting type of writing, there are also some very serious pitfalls you should be aware of *before* you begin to do research. One pitfall is plagiarism.

You must take great care to give credit to the people you cite in your research paper. To present information that someone else has gathered without mentioning that person's name and where the information

came from is to steal that person's work. Similarly, to copy even one sentence from a book or article without putting that sentence into quotation marks is to steal that person's language. Both of these are very serious offenses. A person caught presenting a paper that uses someone else's work without giving that person credit can be expelled from school for plagiarism.

In this chapter, you will learn how to take notes and to cite other people's work so that you will not plagiarize by mistake. If you take notes carefully and document your work as you record the information, you will not find yourself in a situation where you cannot remember where the information came from or whether the notes you have taken are written in your own words or quoted.

Please read the next true story of what happened to a student who was accused of plagiarism at Princeton University. Use the questions on page 117–118 as a guide for your reading.

PLAGIARISM

What You Don't Know Could Hurt You

By Carol Felsenthal

Gabrielle Napolitano's term paper got her into deep trouble. To this day, she insists she should never have been penalized. What do you think?

Twenty-one-year-old Gabrielle Napolitano seemed to have it made. She was one of the top seniors at Princeton, an accomplished athlete and a scholar who had her sights set on law school. Then in February 1982, four months before graduation, a student/faculty discipline committee found her guilty of academia's most serious sin—plagiarism.

Gabrielle was allowed to finish the school year, but as punishment, Princeton withheld her diploma for a year. She waited it out at home in Stamford, Connecticut, working as a noncertified substitute teacher. She had a lot of time that year to wonder if this sole snag in an otherwise impeccable academic record had destroyed her plans to practice law. All six law schools to which she applied rejected her.

How did a girl whose future once seemed so rosy end up in such a bleak predicament?

The January of her senior year, Gabrielle found herself in the classic student bind. After finishing her senior thesis on a Tuesday, she faced a term paper, due Wednesday, on Gabriel García Márquez's novel *One Hundred Years of Solitude*. She stayed up all night to do the paper, wrote the required Princeton pledge—"This paper represents my own work in accordance with university regulations"—at its end, and rushed it to Professor Sylvia Molloy. All the while, she worried about her semester finals—four in six days—which started on Thursday.

The awful news that she had been accused of plagiarism greeted Gabrielle when she returned to Princeton after semester break. Professor Molloy charged her with trying to pass off as her own a paper that had been ". . . lifted, I am afraid, word for word . . ." from a published study of the Márquez novel by Josefina Ludmer.

An examination of Gabrielle's paper seems to confirm the professor's charge. Gabrielle footnoted the Ludmer book a mere five times while using over fifty unacknowledged verbatim or virtually verbatim passages. Professor Molloy's triple-underlined "NO!"—written in red ink next to Gabrielle's pledge of originality—shows how angry and shocked the teacher must have been as she read the paper.

A "TECHNICAL ERROR"?

Gabrielle continues to proclaim her innocence. She insists that she did not intend to plagiarize and that under Princeton's definition of plagiarism— "The *deliberate* [emphasis added] use of any outside source without proper acknowledgment"—she could not be guilty. She contends that the five times she footnoted Ludmer prove she never intended to hide the fact that she used the book. "Professor Molloy herself suggested I use Ludmer in writing this paper. Why in the world would I deliberately plagiarize when I knew she was familiar with the book?" Gabrielle says. If she committed the "technical error" of sometimes "forgetting" to formally footnote, she blames exhaustion and extreme time pressure.

After Princeton's president, William Bowen, denied Gabrielle's appeal for clemency, she took her case to the courts, suing Princeton for damages, claiming "defamation" and "malicious interference" with her ability to pursue a career.

Professors, coaches, and administrators testified to Gabrielle's "unmatched" intellect, achievements, and integrity (one described her as "incapable of intentionally committing the act of plagiarism"). But the trial judge, William Dreier, dismissed Gabrielle's suit on the grounds that the courts should not interfere in the internal affairs of a private university. Her attorney appealed—unsuccessfully. That October, a three-judge panel sustained Judge Dreier's decision. The judge who wrote the opinion seemed appalled by Gabrielle's paper. He denounced it as "a mosaic of the Ludmer work" and "a shoddy attempt" to "pass off" Ludmer's work as her own.

Nathan Edelstein, Gabrielle's attorney, maintains that Princeton's definition of plagiarism is fuzzy. He points to the fact that even Judge Dreier disagreed with the university's interpretation—specifically, on whether intent is relevant to determining guilt. "If the experts can't agree on exactly what plagiarism is, how can a student be expected to know?" Edelstein asks. That's a good question, and the answer is that most students don't know.

CONFLICTING INTERPRETATIONS

Consider the case of Molly, a high school student accused of plagiarizing a paper entitled "Who's to Blame for Pearl Harbor?" Molly merely reworded the ideas of a magazine article on the subject, her history teacher charged, without once giving credit where credit was due. "But I rewrote it. I cut out some stuff and added some new stuff," Molly argued. "That's not plagiarism."

Oh, yes, it is, according to the school's (and the Random House dictionary's) definition of plagiarism: "To steal (the language, ideas, or thoughts) from (another), representing them as one's own original work." The definition simply means that an author's words *and ideas* are his property and anyone who borrows those words or ideas must acknowledge her source.

Definitions of plagiarism and guidelines for acknowledging the use of outside sources vary from school to school and even among departments of the same school. It is the student's responsibility—and hers alone—to get a copy of her school's handbook (most colleges and many high schools have them), to study the section on plagiarism, and to *always* ask individual teachers for their footnoting and quoting requirements.

But there are some cardinal rules to be culled from Gabrielle's and Molly's misfortunes. All students, no matter where they go to school, must remember these principles:

• Intent to plagiarize is irrelevant at most schools, and, in any case, lack of intent is very difficult to prove. You must assume that if what got in your paper was copied from another source that's not acknowledged, you've plagiarized. If you take notes in researching a paper, be sure to carefully note the source of all information—then credit the source for anything you use. The argument "I thought these were my own words, I didn't realize they came from a book" won't wash.
• Claiming "I only copied one sentence here or one paragraph there" is no defense. *Any* uncredited lifting of another person's words or ideas—no matter how small—constitutes plagiarism. In a 1980 survey of students at Iowa State University, in Iowa City, only 44 percent felt it was dishonest to copy a few sentences from a source without footnoting. Yet technically, had that other 56 percent done what they apparently condoned, they would have committed plagiarism.
• "But I put it in my own words" is also no defense. Some students believe that careful paraphrasing gives them carte blanche to plunder another's work. They forget that *ideas* as well as words are the property of the person who created them. Suppose you had devised a theory for a political science term paper on why President Reagan won such a sweeping victory in the last election. Another student read your pa-

115

per and presented the exact theory but in his own words. If he neglected to credit your paper as the source of the idea, he plagiarized.

• You must acknowledge every appearance of borrowed material. Gabrielle was tragically mistaken in thinking that five footnotes would cover fifty borrowed passages.

• Whether or not a source is copyrighted is also immaterial. "Okay, so I copied from a friend's paper," one high school sophomore admitted. "That's not plagiarism. It has never been published; it's not copyrighted." But that student had indeed plagiarized. Unacknowledged borrowing from any outside source—published or unpublished, written by a distinguished authority or by a classmate—is plagiarism. (The student was confusing academic with commercial plagiarism. The latter means stealing from another's published and/or copyrighted material.)

• Remember, keep your school's handbook handy and refer to it as often as necessary. Gabrielle recalls receiving "Rights, Rules, Responsibilities" during her first week at Princeton. She didn't pay much attention to it until she was charged with breaking one of its rules—and by then, it was too late.

• Finally, there is no excuse for plagiarism. Time pressure, conflicting assignments, even a death in the family never justify stealing another's work. Ask the teacher for an extension, no matter how difficult that seems. Confessing your dilemma sure beats risking your reputation and future by resorting to plagiarism out of panic. Gabrielle was understandably embarrassed to ask Professor Molloy for more time. The paper had been assigned during the first class in September and was due any time during the semester but at the latest, on January 13. Gabrielle started the paper on January 12. In retrospect, she wished she had accepted the consequences of a late paper. No matter how severe, they surely could not have been as bad as the consequences with which she must now live.

Despite such harsh consequences, pollsters are finding that increasing numbers of students are taking the risk. In a 1979 survey of Georgia high school students, 78.7 percent of those planning to go to college admitted that they had plagiarized. *Newsweek* reported that in a survey of undergraduates at Stanford University, in California, two thirds confessed to pla-

giarizing papers or padding bibliographies.

Why? When Miami University students were asked why they cheated, 69 percent answered "grade pressure"—many citing the fact that getting into law or medical or business school today requires not just good grades but superlative ones. That pressure is now filtering into the high schools. In a response to a survey in a high school newspaper, the most frequent reason students gave for cheating was "Pressure to get into a good college." "Unless I get into a really first-rate college," one high school junior said, "I can kiss my plans to go to law school good-bye." If a student believes that her future hinges on an A, it is tempting to up the chances of getting one by stealing from an expert.

Increasingly, the cheater is not the marginal student or the student who would rather party than study. She is the academically ambitious person who is determined to grab one of those dwindling spaces in prestigious colleges or professional schools. Sometimes it is the fear that her dishonest classmates will gain a competitive edge in the admissions sweepstakes that makes the basically honest student follow the same course. In a recent survey of medical students, 88 percent admitted to cheating while in college.

Ironically, this intense desire for career success can create a disdain for education. Students go to school not to learn but to get "credentialed." The high school diploma is a "ticket" to an elite college, which in turn is a ticket to graduate school. Whether the tickets are acquired by plagiarizing, by stealing the final, or by working diligently to earn an honest A makes little difference.

Listen to David, who is the only education major in his college fraternity house: "Most of the other guys are business or accounting jocks. They want to get out and make money. They just don't care," he adds, as he describes the various cheating aids available to members, including a hoard of stolen exams and a stable of "ringers"—bright students who will take exams for ill-prepared "brothers."

Jeremy, a business major and David's fraternity brother, explains why he handed in a paper from his frat's well-stocked file of term papers. "I'm preparing for the real world. Business is unethical. Cheating in college is just good training. I'll be better able to handle what's put at me when I get out."

Marsha's dishonesty is an expression of another sort of contempt for education. A sophomore at a large suburban high school, Marsha claims that she cheats "to protest the very low level of teaching." She started out by copying from the *World Book Encyclopedia* but soon graduated to more obscure sources. "I've never been caught," Marsha says proudly. A look of embarrassment crosses her face but only fleetingly. "What's the difference?" she concludes. "I'll bet you that these days, everybody cheats."

CASUAL ATTITUDES

Unfortunately, statistics confirm Marsha's hunch. In 1969, 30.4 percent of a sample of Georgia high school students agreed with the statement "Sometimes it is necessary to be dishonest." By 1979, that figure had soared to 62.4 percent when the same question was put to a new crop of college-bound students. Students today seem to simply accept cheating as part of "the game," as something "everyone does." The only sin is getting caught.

One of the questions on the previously mentioned high school newspaper survey was "Have you ever cheated in any way on your schoolwork?" Eighty-four percent answered yes, but more significantly, 57 percent of the respondents said they never felt guilty about cheating. In a nationwide survey of high school students conducted by the University of Michigan's Institute for Social Research, 75.2 percent said they would not care if their classmates cheated. A professor at Bloomsburg State College, in Pennsylvania, got similar results. Seventy-five percent of the students he surveyed considered cheating a normal part of life. Only one of the 1,500 respondents in the Iowa State University survey mentioned earlier said he would report a fellow student for cheating.

That students' attitudes toward cheating are so casual is not surprising. Most figure they won't get caught, and if they do, well, punishment for plagiarism has been relatively mild—a failing grade on the paper or, at worst, in the course. At least that's how it has been until now.

Colleges and even high schools are beginning to crack down, as Gabrielle learned from sad experience. A one-year suspension is Princeton's standard punishment for plagiarism. Worst of all, the conviction remains on the student's transcript to plague him or her with every graduate school or job application. One high school in a suburb of Cleveland has established a hot line for students to report cheaters. That school, and many others across the nation, gives cheaters an X grade, which remains on their permanent records as a red flag to college-admissions people.

Linda, a Philadelphia teenager, believes that an X grade cost her her rightful place at an Ivy League school. "I was caught plagiarizing in the spring of my junior year," she explains, "and I just couldn't get my English teacher to forget it just that once. My high school transcript showed all A's, except for two B's and that X. That X did me in. Otherwise, I'm sure I would have gotten in anywhere. Two other kids at my school whose grades and activities weren't nearly as good as mine got into Harvard."

Because Linda had only applied to the cream of the college crop, her unexpected rejections left her scrambling to get into a community college. She is very unhappy. "All those years of striving for A's. Then one mistake, and presto, all anybody remembers about me is that I'm a plagiarist."

The same fear haunts Gabrielle Napolitano. She is still living at home with her parents, working and going to school part-time to study business administration and trying to put the sad past behind her.

Source: Carol Felsenthal, "Plagiarism—What You Don't Know Could Hurt You," *Seventeen Magazine,* May 1985, p. 179.

Discussion Questions

1. In your own words, define plagiarism.
2. Why is plagiarism a serious offense?

3. What can happen to a student who is caught plagiarizing?
4. What mistake did Molly and Gabrielle make?
5. Do you think they were guilty? Why or why not?
6. What would happen to someone who did this in your school?
7. What should a student do to avoid any possibility of plagiarizing?

Gathering Information

One of the most important aspects of writing a research paper is the actual research. Your ability to take accurate notes and to document your notes systematically is crucial if you are going to write a well-documented paper.

Gathering information can be done in a variety of ways. One way is to write information on note cards. Another way is to photocopy all or part of your source at the library and then write the citation on each page you have copied. Some people prefer to borrow all the material they plan to use and then to put slips of paper into the book at the pages they wish to cite. In this section, we will discuss each of these information gathering techniques so that you can begin *Writing Your Way*.

SOME COMMONLY ASKED QUESTIONS

Students usually have many questions about citing information. Here are some frequently asked questions. If you have others, ask your instructor or consult a research book which deals specifically with research methods.

1. What is a citation?

A citation tells the reader where you got the information. It gives the reader sufficient information so that, if interested, the reader can go to the library and easily locate the information in its original form.

2. What does a citation look like?

There are several acceptable forms of citations. Consult a reference book that clearly shows you how to document for a book, article, encyclopedia, a journal, or an unpublished work. In this book, we will give you some of the basic forms, but you will need to refer to the Modern Language Association (MLA) or American Psychological Association (APA) guide when you do in-depth research.

A sample bibliographical citation for a book with two authors would look like this:

Genzel, Rhona, and Martha Cummings, *Culturally Speaking*, New York: Harper & Row, 1986.

3. Is there more than one acceptable footnote format?

There are several recognized formats for presenting information. The most frequently used are the MLA (Modern Language Association) and the APA (The American Psychological Association). In this book, we will use the MLA format of parenthetical footnotes.

4. What information should I cite?

You must cite:

a. Quoted material
b. Graphs, charts, photographs, illustrations, tables
c. Ideas, theories, or philosophies that are attributed to someone

You do not have to cite information that is considered common knowledge. Common knowledge information is information that most people in your field know. It is information that is a fact or that you can read about in many places. For example, that President John F. Kennedy was assassinated in Dallas, Texas, is such a fact.

5. What is the purpose of a bibliography? How do I prepare one?

The bibliography provides the reader with an alphabetical listing, by the authors' last names, of the sources you have used to write your research paper. If you write your sources on index cards as you do your research, all you will have to do is put them in alphabetical order by author and type them.

6. What information do I have to include in each entry in the bibliography? Is special punctuation required?

Each entry begins with the author's last name, followed by a comma, the author's first name which is also followed by a comma, and the title of the book which should be underlined. Next write the city where the book was published and the copyright date. (See model under question 2.)

7. Why do I have to underline the title? I thought I could use quotation marks.

You are partially right. If the title appears on the cover of the book, you must underline it. If the title is the name of an article or chapter in a book or magazine, you must underline the title of the book or magazine and put quotation marks around the name of the chapter or article. Here is an example:

Source: Rebecca Oxford-Carpenter, "Second Language Learning Strategies: What the Research Has to Say," ERIC/CLL News Bulletin, September 9, 1985.

Information-Gathering Methods

PHOTOCOPYING

Some researchers like to photocopy the material they intend to use from journals and other sources they cannot borrow from the library. In this way, they have the entire article at home to use as they construct their research paper.

There are some drawbacks to this method, however. Photocopying quantities of material can be very expensive. The researcher must also take care to write all the bibliographic information directly on each page of the article when it is photocopied. This way, the writer will have the citation material readily available. Failure to do this, however, may cost the researcher an additional trip to the library to relocate the source or may result in a citation error.

USING INDEX CARDS

In this method, researchers locate the sources they need to gather information. Then they write each source on a separate card. Note the order in which information is presented and the punctuation that is used.

SAMPLE BIBLIOGRAPHY CARD

Fowler, H. Ramsey, *The Little Brown Handbook* 3 ed. Boston: Little, Brown and Company, 1986.

Remember to write only *one* book or magazine on a card. When you write your research paper, you simply alphabetize these cards and type them exactly as they appear, in alphabetical order, on the last page of your research paper.

As mentioned earlier, there are two major forms used for writing citations: MLA and APA. Use a handbook that lists the ways to cite information and follow it for each type of publication you wish to include in your research.

NOW YOU DO IT

Practice Writing Citations

Below is a list of all the data you will need to write a citation. However, it is not correctly ordered or punctuated. Use this information to write a complete citation. Ask your instructor to check your work when you finish.

1. *People Types and Tiger Stripes*
   G. D. Lawrence
   1982
   Gainesville, Florida
   Center for Applications of Psychological Type

   _____

   _____

   _____

2. Elwood Murray
   The Speech Personality: Integration of the Speaker
   Chicago
   J. B. Lippincott Publisher
   1937

   _____

   _____

   _____

3. *Psychological Types*
   New York
   Harcourt Brace Publishers, Inc.
   C. G. Jung
   1923

   _____

   _____

   _____

4. Regents Publishing Co.
   New York
   Inside English
   Virginia French Allen
   1983

   _____

   _____

   _____

NOTE TAKING

After you locate your sources, the next step is to read the material and to take notes. Note taking can be done in a variety of ways: *summarizing, paraphrasing,* or *synthesizing.* Remember to include only one piece of information per card. Notes should be taken on either 3″ × 5″ or 5″ × 7″ index cards.

SUMMARIZING

A summary is used when you want to state only the essence of a chapter or article in your own words. To write the summary, first locate the main idea. This is what the article is about. Then identify the ideas that support the main idea. The final step is to condense this information into one to four sentences.

Read the sample article and the answers to the questions which follow. Notice how the writer has summarized the information on the sample note card.

RIPE IDEA

New Robot Able to Spot Fruit Ready for Picking

Mount Dora, Fla.—(AP)—A new robot that can spot fruit on a tree, determine its ripeness and even pluck it could revolutionize the harvesting of oranges and other fruit, a University of Florida researcher says.

Using the latest robotics, computer and sensing technology, scientists have developed an "intelligent" mechanical picker, said Dr. Roy C. Harrell, an assistant professor at the university's Institute of Food and Agricultural Sciences.

A color television camera on the end of a picking arm finds orange-colored or ripe fruit on a tree, and a sonar sensing unit provides the computer with information on the distance between the fruit and the tip of the picking arm.

When contact is made, a lip rotates behind the fruit and severs the stem, allowing the fruit to drop into a collection bin.

With at least six and as many as 12 picking arms, a commercial robot harvester under ideal operating conditions would be able to harvest six pieces of fruit per second, Harrell said. A single operator would be needed to position the harvester next to a row of trees.

Source: *Miami Herald,* Section B, December 29, 1987, p. 5. Reprinted by permission of the Associated Press.

Questions:

1. What is the main idea of the article?

   High technology robots can be used to pick fruit.

2. Give three details that support the main idea.

   a. Color TV camera locates the fruit.

   b. Sonar sensor provides information on distance of fruit

   from the picking arm.

c. <u>Robots can pick six pieces of fruit per second.</u>

3. Write the main idea and the three supporting points in one sentence.

   <u>Robots equipped with a color TV camera, picking arm, and</u>

   <u>sonar sensor can pick six pieces of fruit per second.</u>

4. Write this sentence on the notecard below. Provide complete citation information including the page number and name of the source.

Miami Herald	p. 5B
August 15, 1987	
Robots equipped with a color TV camera, a picking arm, and	
a sonar sensor, can pick six pieces of fruit per second.	

NOW YOU DO IT

Read each article and answer the questions which follow.

Article 1:

MACHINE TO BLAST GALLSTONES AWAY

Large-scale testing will begin soon to discover whether shock-wave machines can replace surgery for victims of gallstones, just as the procedure has revolutionized treatment of kidney stones, experts say.

The machine, called a lithotripter, uses shock waves to smash stones in the body. Since it was introduced in the United States about four years ago, it has become the accepted treatment for kidney stones, which had required about 130,000 operations annually.

Now, experts hope a modified version of the machine will do something similar for gallstones, which are 10 times more common than kidney stones. Although gallstones often cause no problems, 400,000 to 550,000 Americans undergo gallstone surgery annually.

"There is every reason to expect that we may be looking at a new standard of care," Dr. Randolph B. Reinhold of New England Medical Center said this week.

He predicted that it may be useful for as many as half the gallstone sufferers who now need surgery.

Source: "Machine Blasts Gallstones Away," *Rochester Democrat and Chronicle,* Frontiers Section, August 15, 1987, p. 7C. Reprinted by permission of Gannett Rochester Newspapers.

Questions:

1. What new procedure will be tested?

_____

_____

_____

2. What has this procedure been used on before?

_____

_____

_____

3. What is the name of the machine?

_____

_____

_____

4. How many people require surgery for this problem every year?

_____

_____

_____

5. What is Dr. Reinhold's prediction?

_____

_____

_____

6. Combine your answers into two or three sentences. Write them and the citation information on the note card below:

Article 2:

BIGGEST RISE IN 15 MONTHS

The Associated Press

Output at the nation's factories, mines and utilities, boosted by a rebound in oil and gas drilling and higher production at auto plants, surged 0.8 percent in July, the biggest increase in 15 months.

The Federal Reserve yesterday said the increase in industrial production, the sixth in a row, followed upward revisions in the last three months. The June increase was boosted to 0.4 percent, instead of an originally reported 0.2 percent gain.

"Industrial production continues to rise, providing a strong degree of optimism for the underlying strength of the economy," White House spokesman Martin Fitzwater said in Santa Barbara, Calif., where President Reagan is vacationing.

Analysts credited the upturn to a steady rise in American export sales overseas.

"The industrial output figures are bigger than I thought they would be.

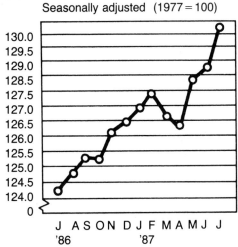

U.S. Industrial Production Index
Seasonally adjusted (1977 = 100)

J A S O N D J F M A M J J
'86   '87

Source of data: Federal Reserve Board

They are another signal of the strength of the economy," said Lawrence Kudlow, chief economist for Bear, Stearns & Co. of New York.

Source: Rochester Democrat and Chronicle, August 15, 1987, Section D, p. 7D. Reprinted by permission of the Associated Press.

Questions:

1. What happened in July?

_____

_____

2. Why is this important? Give two reasons.

_____

_____

_____

125

3. Summarize this information on the note card below:

Article 3:

Using the same concept, read the article "Car Manufacturers Ponder What's in a Name" on page 128. Determine the main idea and the information that supports or proves the idea. Then summarize this information in three or four sentences on the note card below. Provide correct citations.

CAR MANUFACTURERS PONDER WHAT'S IN A NAME

"You might not want a car named Dog or Warthog—and that's why we never see such names."

By Richard Wright

Are the automakers running out of car names? If not, why are we getting names like Allante (Cadillac) and Reatta (Buick)? Unlike Impala or Mustang or Monza, these new names have no meaning; they are made up.

Making up names for cars is nothing new, of course (Chevelle, Corvair, Chevette, Toronado, for example). These words are relatively neutral, whereas names that already exist have meanings and connotations.

Automakers don't just take any name that comes along to put on a new car, they choose very carefully (usually).

For example, they suspect you might not want a car named Dog or Warthog—and that's why we never see such names. Mustang or Thunderbird, sure, but probably not Hyena or Buzzard.

Would you buy a car with a name like Mongoose Civique or Utopian Turtletop? Ford Motor Co. was dubious and rejected these suggestions from poet Marianne Moore in favor of Edsel. Didn't buy that either, eh?

Going with the name of the boss is in the auto industry's tradition, as most names of car lines are those of the man who made the car. Thus, we have rolling reminders of Henry Ford, David Buick, Ransom Olds, Louis Chevrolet, Walter P. Chrysler and John and Horace Dodge, automotive pioneers all.

From Europe (and, for a while, Wisconsin), nameplates remind us of Louis Renault, Armand Peugeot, Karl Benz, Gottlieb Daimler, Adam Opel, C. S. Rolls, and Henry Royce, Ferdinand Porsche (who designed the Volkswagen), Herbert Austin, Andre Citroen, the Maserati brothers and Enzo Ferrari.

The Honda perpetuates the name of one of Japan's great automotive figures, Soichiro Honda, and with a slight change Toyota carries the name of its founding family, Toyoda.

Detroit automotive pioneer Henry Leland named the cars he created after heroes from history, Antoine de Le Mothe Cadillac, founder of Detroit, and President Abraham Lincoln.

The remaining Big Three car lines are Mercury, named for the Roman God; Plymouth, apparently named with Plymouth Rock in mind; and Pontiac, named for the city in which it is built. Other cars also bear place names: Monte Carlo, Malibu, Monterey, Torino, LeMans, Riviera, Versailles, Aspen, Daytona, Capri, Calais, Granada, Bel Air and Biscayne. One even has the name of a mythical place, Eldorado.

Some makers carry the name of their factory, such as BMW, which means Bavarian Motor Works. Fiat started as an acronym for Italian words that meant "Italian automobile factory in Turin."

Government officials have enjoyed periods of automotive popularity, Nash had its Statesman and Ambassador, the latter revived by American Motors Corp. Dodge marketed a Diplomat for a while and Studebaker offered the President and the Commander. It also offered a Dictator for a while in the '30s, until it became clear that dictators were not to be well thought of.

Animals have always been popular: Mustang, Maverick, Pinto, Cougar, Bobcat, Lynx, Jaguar—as have fish: Barracuda, Marlin, Sting Ray—and birds: Falcon, Lark, Skylark, Hawk, Skyhawk, Eagle and those legendary birds, Thunderbird, Sunbird, Firebird, and Phoenix.

There have been some odd names, however: A company in the village of Owego, near Binghamton, built the O-We-Go in 1914. And in Detroit, Autoparts Manufacturing Co. introduced a car in 1912 called the Dodo.

It never got off the ground.

Source: Wright, Richard, "Car Manufacturers Ponder What's in a Name," *Rochester Democrat and Chronicle,* August 15, 1987, p. 8D. Reprinted by permission of the Gannett News Service.

PARAPHRASING

Paraphrasing is another technique used to take research notes. In paraphrasing, the researcher restates, in his or her own words, what the author has said.

When you are taking notes, you can use paraphrasing to restate a sentence or group of sentences. Please read the paragraph that follows and write a paraphrase on the lines below.

The wiring in our school was old, and on this particular day, we suffered a power outage in some of the buildings. The administration did not want to cancel classes even though there was no electricity. Professors continued to teach and students continued to take notes and exams as scheduled. Toward the end of the day, a young, very upset international student came into my office. It seemed that she had just taken her first college math exam in the dark. She told me she had heard that cheating was a problem in the United States, but she didn't know that the professor would turn off the lights during the exam!

SYNTHESIZING

To synthesize is to combine the information gathered from two or more sources. Synthesizing requires the skills you have learned in paraphrasing and summarizing as well as the ability to see the relationship between ideas, materials, or events.

To see how synthesis works, read the articles and answer the questions below.

LANGUAGE KEYBOARD

Grace Marie Raynor, a retired school teacher who lives in Newhall, Calif., has invented a communications process described as useful in teaching English as a second language and overcoming illiteracy. Patent 4,684,348, granted her this week, describes a keyboard with numerals alone or numerals with letters.

This, she said by telephone, creates a universal alphabet that can be translated into various languages.

Source: Rochester Democrat and Chronicle, August 15, 1987, p. 11D.

Questions:

1. What is the main idea of this article?

_____

_____

_____

2. How does the keyboard work?

_____

_____

_____

CHINESE CHARACTERS IN COMPUTERS

A system for encoding Chinese characters, and a keyboard for such use, were patented this week by Wang Yong-Min of the Computation Center in Henan Province [sic], China. According to patent 4,484,926, Chinese characters and phrases can be stored in computers of any size, as well as in systems for Chinese information processing and communications.

The Chinese characters are to be broken down into "roots" which are arranged on a standard keyboard. The operator is said to be able to key in texts at a speed from 120 to 150 characters per minute without looking at the keyboard.

Source: Stacy V. Jones, "Patents: Chinese Characters Encoded for Computers," *The New York Times,* August 8, 1987. Copyright © 1987 by The New York Times Company. Reprinted by permission.

Questions:

1. What is the main idea of this article?

_____

_____

_____

2. How does the computer work?

_____

_____

_____

_____

_____

_____

Application Synthesis:

You have to write a research paper on how computers can be used in teaching language. Combine the information from the two articles to explain the computer's importance in language learning.

_____

_____

_____

_____

_____

_____

_____

_____

_____

QUOTING

Quote material when you copy the exact words of the author. Place a quotation mark (") both before and after the quoted material. Your note card would look like this:

Cummings, Martha G. *Half Lives*, New York: Better Ideas
Press, 1988.
"To succeed in the paperwork jungle, an employee must have
the ability to wrap his eccentricities about him like a cloak
and slip unnoticed to the document shredder." p. 127

Some people code all their bibliography cards by putting a letter of the alphabet in the corner of each card. Then, when they prepare their notecards, instead of writing the complete citation, they write only the code for that book, the page number, and the quote or paraphrase. Their card would look like this:

			C
			p 127
"To succeed in the paperwork jungle, an employee must have			
the ability to wrap his eccentricities about him like a cloak			
and slip unnoticed to the document shredder."			

In this chapter, you have learned to:

☐ Summarize or condense.
☐ Paraphrase or restate.
☐ Synthesize by combining elements from different articles to create a whole.
☐ Quote or use exact words.

In the following exercise, you will use all these techniques.

NOW YOU DO IT

You have an assignment to investigate euthanasia or "mercy killing" and write a persuasive essay expressing your opinion. Do the following:

1. Read the three articles which follow and take notes. You may either:
   a. Underline the important points in the articles.
   b. Write separate note cards using summary, synthesis, quotations, and paraphrasing.
   c. Photocopy the articles. Then cut them up and paste the information you intend to use on note cards.
2. Use the organizational matrix page 137 to organize your information and to guide your writing.
3. Write one sentence that expresses your opinion of euthanasia.
4. List three or four reasons that support your opinions. Use data from the articles to reenforce or illustrate these reasons.
5. Write an essay using this information.
6. Write a bibliography listing the sources you refer to in your essay.
7. If you prefer to write your essay first, use the matrix to check it. By filling in the boxes with the main ideas you used and the details used to support each, you have a handy method to check the content and organization of your essay.

SENILITY ISN'T A CAPITAL OFFENSE

By Ellen Goodman

Some have called it a Right to Die case. Others have labelled it a Right to Live case.

One group of advocates has called for death with dignity. Others have responded accusingly, euthanasia.

At the center of the latest controversy about life and death, medicine and law, is a 78-year-old Massachusetts man whose existence hangs on a court order.

On one point, everyone agrees: Earle Spring is not the man he used to be.

Once a strapping outdoorsman, he now is strapped to a wheelchair. Once a man with a keen mind, he now is called senile by many, and mentally incompetent by the courts.

He is, at worst, a member of the living dead; at best, a shriveled version of his former self.

For more than two years, since his physical and then mental health began to deteriorate, Earle Spring has been kept alive by spending five hours on a kidney dialysis machine three times a week. Since January 1979, his family has pleaded to have him removed from the life support system.

They believe deeply that the Earle Spring who was, would not want to live as the Earle Spring who is. They believe they are advocates for his right to die in peace.

In the beginning, the courts agreed. Possibly for the first time, they ruled last month in favor of withdrawing medical care from an elderly patient whose mind had deteriorated. The dialysis was stopped.

But then, in a sudden intervention, an outside nurse and doctor visited Earle Spring and testified that he was alert enough to make a weak expression of his desire to live. And so the treatments resumed.

Now, while the courts are waiting for new and more thorough evidence about Spring's mental state, the controversy rages about legal procedures. No judge ever visited Spring, no psychiatrist ever testified. And even more importantly, we again are forced to determine one person's right to die or to live.

This case makes the Karen Ann Quinlan story seem simple in comparison. Quinlan today hangs onto her life long after her plug was pulled. But when the New Jersey court heard that case, Quinlan had no will. She had suffered brain death by any definition.

The Spring story is different. He is neither competent nor comatose. He lives in a gray area of consciousness. So the questions also range over the gray area of our consciences.

What should the relationship be between mental health and physical treatment? Should we treat the incompetent as aggressively as the competent?

Should we order heart surgery for one senile citizen; should we take another off a kidney machine? What is the mental line between a life worth saving and the living dead? Who is to decide?

Until recently, we didn't have the technology to keep an Earle Spring alive.

Until recently the life-and-death decisions about the senile elderly or the retarded or the institutionalized were made privately between families and medical people. Now, increasingly, in states like Massachusetts, they are made publicly and legally.

Clearly there are no absolutes in this case. No right to die. No right to live. We have to take into account many social as well as medical factors.

How much of the resources of a society or a family should be allotted to a member who no longer recognizes it? How many sacrifices should the healthy and vital make for the terminally or permanently ill and disabled?

In England, where kidney dialysis machines are scarce, Earle Spring would never have remained on one. In America, one Earle Spring can decimate the energy and income of an entire family.

But the Spring case is a crucial, scary one that could affect all those living under that dubious sentence, incompetent, or that shaky diagnosis, senile.

So, it seems to me that if there is one moment a week when the fog lifts, and when this man wants to live, if there is any mental activity at all, then disconnecting him from life would be a dangerous precedent, far more dangerous than letting him continue.

The court ruled originally in favor of taking Spring off the machine. It ruled that this is what Earle Spring would have wanted. I have no doubt that his family believes it. I have no doubt of their affection or their pain.

But I remember, too, what my grandfather used to say: "No one wants to live to be 100 until you ask the man who is 99."

Well, no one, including Earle Spring, wants to live to be senile. But, once senile, he may well want to live. We simply have to give him the benefit of the doubt. Any doubt.

LIVING WILL—THE RIGHT TO DIE

To: My Family, My Executor, My Physician and My Lawyer:

If the time comes when I can no longer take part in decisions for my own future, I want you to be guided by this expression of my views.

If there is no reasonable expectation of my recovery from physical or mental disability, I request that I be allowed to die, preferably at home, and that no artificial means or heroic measures be employed to prolong my life. Death is as much a reality as birth, growth, maturity and old age. I do not fear death as much as I fear the indignity of deterioration, dependence and hopeless pain. I ask that drugs be mercifully administered to me for terminal suffering even if they hasten the moment of death. I have no desire to be kept alive by machines in a hospital if there is no sound medical hope of a recovery which will permit me to participate meaningfully in life.

The language quoted above is a good example of a "Living Will," sometimes referred to as a "Right to Die" statement or a "Death with Dignity" declaration. The development of such documents has been stimulated by modern medical techniques and devices. Artificial respirators, mechanical heart pumps and intravenous feedings can extend the life of a patient's body long after "brain death" has occurred.

The medical and legal professions and the courts are working to find an acceptable definition of death. One thoughtful physician, Dr. Donald W. Seldin (Chairman, Department of Internal Medicine, Southwestern Medical School, University of Texas), observes that there are three levels of life: (1) biochemical life, in which the metabolic processes of a cell are intact; (2) vegetative life, in which the functions of the organs and organ systems are intact; and, (3) human life, in which there is the capacity of intentionality and purposeful behavior. Dr. Seldin suggests that if a person has irretrievably lost the capacity of human life, the situation may be an appropriate one for carrying out the Living Will. The decision would be made jointly by the person's family and physician.

If a person wishes to have a Living Will, he or she should sign and execute the document with the same formalities used for a Will disposing of property.

Living Wills today are legally questionable. Many lawyers and doctors are rightfully concerned about charges of malpractice and even criminal conduct if every effort to extend and preserve life is not pursued.

Some states are struggling to create laws to deal with these issues. The Karen Ann Quinlan case is an example of the many legal, moral and ethical problems involved. Some people believe it would be wise to continue to rely on the good sense and compassion of families and doctors rather than writing detailed rules and regulations on the right to die. Each of us, while in good health, should discuss these questions calmly and reflectively with our loved ones.

Source: "Living Will—The Right to Die," from *The Ann Landers Encyclopedia A to Z.* Copyright © 1978 by Esther P. Lederer. Reprinted by permission of Doubleday, a division of Bantam, Doubleday, Dell Publishing Group, Inc. Credit: Newton N. Minow, Attorney, Chicago, Illinois.

Pat O'Brien on CBS *Spectrum* radio program said the following:

Finally a case has surfaced that points to the terrible risks involved when doctors and families exercise the power to determine an individual's right to live or die. Earle Spring of Massachusetts, a 78-year-old man ruled mentally incompetent by the courts, was kept alive only by spending many hours on a kidney dialysis machine three days a week.

Last month his family persuaded the court that Spring would want to die if he were competent enough to express his wishes. They asked for and were granted a ruling stopping the dialysis treatment. They said they want Spring to die in peace, with dignity. The problem is Earle Spring never told anyone he wanted that particular privilege. To the contrary, he whispered to his nurses that he did not want to die. The nurses said publicly they were appalled at the court decision. The court quickly reversed itself and Earle Spring was put back on dialysis treatment.

The subsequent public uproar has been like touching a match to gasoline. Once again the troubling questions of who decides when to pull the plug and end another human being's life are surfacing and still there are no easy answers.

The machines of modern medicine present us with choices we never had before. Families watching someone they love shrink slowly towards death are often caught by soaring hospital bills wanting with all their hearts the sadness to be over.

From this has come the Right to Die Movement, an effort to provide a chosen option when normal life is no longer possible. But Earle Spring is no Carol Ann Quinlan. He does not live as does she as a vegetable with no brain function. His case is scary, different and important.

The will to live is an awesome thing. We need only consider the endurance of concentration camp inmates or the fight of a cancer victim to get a glimpse of what power that will holds. And no one has the right to trample on it, as long as there is a flicker of mental activity.

In my opinion, the courts should never have stopped dialysis treatment for Earle Spring. That's not the power I would want them to have if I were the one in that hospital bed. No one, I fervently hope, will ever say that I want the right to die, unless I have told them so first. I wish nothing less for anyone else. I'm Pat O'Brien for Spectrum.

Six personal points of view on Spectrum—opinions not necessarily those of *CBS* Radio *Network*.

Source: Pat O'Brien, *Spectrum*, transcript of 1980 radio broadcast reprinted by permission of CBS News.

Matrix for Essay on Euthanasia

Topic: _____

Thesis Sentence: _____

_____

**Sentence of
Method:** _____

_____

Attention-Getting Sentence: _____

_____

MAIN IDEAS	SUPPORTING DETAILS

Nine

Writing the Mini Research Paper

Source: Charles Schulz, *Peanuts.* Reprinted by permission of UFS, Inc.

Many students feel the same way Lucy does about research papers. However, since college students can't get away with "writing big," they must take the alternative of doing "hard research."

As we've discussed previously, research is the investigation of a subject to learn or to collect data to support an idea. The research paper is the written presentation of this information. Because the research paper includes the ideas and thoughts of others, the writer must give credit to his or her sources in the bibliography and footnotes.

In the previous chapter, we studied note taking, summarizing, paraphrasing, and synthesizing information. In this chapter, you will use the resources provided to write a mini research paper. This will involve:

- ☐ Analyzing material for main ideas and supporting details
- ☐ Taking notes on written material
- ☐ Drawing conclusions
- ☐ Deciding on a thesis or main idea, supporting ideas, and details or examples
- ☐ Organizing your material
- ☐ Presenting your findings in written form

☐ Using footnotes
☐ Preparing a bibliography
☐ Incorporating quoted material

Follow the directions carefully. Approach the research paper as a challenging opportunity to learn and to share new information rather than as an onerous task. If you see the positives, you'll find you get the full enjoyment from assignments.

COMBINING THE ESSAY WITH RESEARCH

In this chapter we will combine the information you have learned about writing an essay with what you learned in Chapter Eight about taking notes.

On a separate sheet of paper, *write* (do not print) the following sentences:

Writing a research paper takes time and energy. The writer must be thoroughly familiar with the subject to do a good job.

Put your name at the top of the paper and give it to your instructor. Your instructor will then distribute the papers so each student has a paper written by a classmate.

Look at your classmate's paper. Your job will be to analyze the writer's handwriting. To do this, you must do some research on graphoanalysis. Information on graphoanalysis is provided for you in the articles which follow.

Your teacher may have you write the sample sentences above and then begin the reading and note taking in class. Depending on the length of the class period, you may have to complete the reading and note taking at home. In the next class session, you will begin the writing stage.

Reading Reference Material

NOW YOU DO IT

In the previous chapter you learned how to take notes. In this chapter you will have an opportunity to practice this skill and apply it toward writing a mini research paper or annotated essay.

Read the articles that follow and take notes on notecards. It is best to use cards that are 3″ × 5″ or 5″ × 7″. Remember to prepare bibliography cards too.

1. Read the articles on handwriting.
2. Take notes on note cards or paper that is approximately 5″ × 7″.
3. You will need information on handwriting analysis in general. This is provided for you in the articles. This information will be used to write your introduction.

4. Read how the experts analyze handwriting. Compare the letters discussed in the article with those in the writing sample you are to analyze.
5. Think about the information you have gathered. What does it tell you?
6. Remember to use correct citations both on your note cards and in your mini research paper.
7. Have your instructor check your note cards before you begin to organize and write your mini research paper.

JUDGING A JOB SEEKER BY THE CROSS OF HIS "T"

"T" BAR INTERPRETATIONS

_____ indicates enthusiasm, follow-through and a person who will get the job done.

_____ indicates a person with enthusiasm, but ambitions higher than his / her potential

_____ shows procrastination.

_____ indicates a person who has high goals, but lacks enthusiasm.

_____ the cup indicates shallow purpose.

_____ the "T" bar compared to bending a steel bar. The person is trying very hard to keep something under control.

_____ the tent-like stem indicates stubborness.

Source: Management World, March 1978.

Source: " 'T' Bar Interpretations," *New York Times*, January 30, 1980. Copyright © 1980 by The New York Times Company. Reprinted by permission.

If you cross your "t's" with sky-high strokes, you're a dreamer. If the loops of your "d's" are capacious enough to contain tea for two, you're a sensitive soul. If your capital "p's" start with a left hook that would knock Joe Frazier flat, you're a bit materialistic.

It may sound like a familiar parlor game, but some people take it much more seriously. Handwriting analysis, that tenuous art of minding everyone else's "p's" and "q's," has changed its name to graphoanalysis, and it's etching a place for itself in the personnel department.

Used throughout history to verify the authenticity of signatures and documents, handwriting analysis, or graphology, some say, is a valid means to disclose the personality behind the scribbles as well.

Shelia Kurtz, a graphoanalyst for the last 10 years, has built a successful company on that belief. New Slant Inc., at 110 Riverside Drive in Manhattan, has a growing number of clients—large companies and small—who use handwriting analyses of job candidates as part of the interviewing process.

"Our slogan is 'Handwriting is brain writing,'" says Mrs. Kurtz, who has a background in psychology. "We believe that the pen is mightier than the personnel interview."

Mary Anne Sommers, now national sales manager for Art News and Antiques World magazines, hired the advertising sales staff of her former employer, Working Woman magazine, based on handwriting evaluations by Mrs. Kurtz.

"We asked the applicants," Miss

Sommers said, "if they would object to a handwriting analysis, and a few looked at me askance, but everyone did it. And I put together an absolutely dynamite sales staff; they were all women and they were terrific."

Since then, Miss Sommers and most of her sales staff have "moved on to bigger and better places," she said. But the new management at Working Woman no longer uses handwriting analysis in its interviewing process. "They thought it was hocus-pocus," Miss Sommers said. "They didn't want me to talk about it."

Indeed, most companies that use handwriting analysis in hiring don't talk about it. "That's just the nature of the business," Mrs. Kurtz said. "It's confidential.

The fact that different handwriting strokes can mean "failing" a job interview hasn't generated any legal challenges thus far.

According to Jack Novik, a lawyer for the American Civil Liberties-Union in New York, no legal action has been brought against the practice.

Nonetheless, there is a widespread sense of caution about the use of handwriting analysis for hiring purposes. Donald Lott, a spokesman for the Equal Employment Opportunity Commission in Washington, noted that the practice "falls under the commission's policy with regard to testing."

"If that testing has a disproportionate impact in terms of its effect on certain classes of individuals and if those persons raise allegations of racial, sexual or other discrimination," Mr. Lott said, "the testing facility stands to be exposed to the enforcement authority of the commission."

Graphoanalysis, a specialized outgrowth of the study of handwriting, was developed around 50 years ago by Milton Newman Bunker, a shorthand expert, chiropractor and founder of the International Graphoanalysis Society. It combines the study of various factors—slant, pressure and strokes—to assess the character of the writer. Slant is measured by a gauge with various emotive connotations, ranging from "extreme withdrawal" (far to the left) to "extremely responsive" (far to the right). T-bars, t-stems, size of loops and end strokes are basic indicators, as are the size of letters and the heaviness of the pressure.

The society is quick to point out that "there is no validity in the belief that a single graphic sign denotes the existence of a specific trait," according to Lucille Range, director of public affairs. All elements are evaluated as a whole, and single traits may be offset or diminished by others. A prospective employee's compatibility with established workers is often an important consideration.

Felix Klein, of Manhattan Handwriting Consultants, 250 West 57th Street, practices graphology, not Graphoanalysis. The former, he says, involves "the Gestalt method, meaning the overall character structure." His company has been involved in personnel selection for 56 years.

"It's a very simple procedure and a very effective one," Mr. Klein said. "We have constant feedback from our clients."

Both Mr. Klein and Mrs. Kurtz say that their evaluations of a job candidate are sometimes not counted at all, and are never the entire basis for a hiring decision. The analysis is used in conjunction with the job interview and is evaluated along with the applicant's experience and skills.

Herry O. Teltscher, a clinical psychologist and practicing graphologist, said he has a dozen clients who use handwriting analysis in hiring, some of whom have been using the method for 20 years. His analyses, he said, focus on the positive characteristics of the applicant.

There are two other Manhattan handwriting analysts that advertise personnel selection services. Fees range from $50 to $300, depending on the depth and detail of the analysis.

Analyze Your Handwriting (and everyone else's!)

How much do you reveal every time you leave a note or write a letter? It may be more than just the words on the page.

by Joyce Dyer

When most of us think of handwriting analysis, we probably think of a machine at a fair or amusement park. Sandwiched between the cotton-candy stand and the beanbag toss is the handwriting booth. You feed your signature into the computer, and instant results spill out, accompanied by flashing lights and the whir of a busy motor.

Graphology, the study of character through handwriting, deserves much more than this sideshow reputation. It's not a matter of magic or of "fortune-telling": In the unique lines of each person's script lie clues to his or her personality.

It's hard to think of a profession that doesn't use the knowledge of graphology in some way. The International Graphoanalysis Society estimates that more than 1,500 American firms employ handwriting consultants to help with hiring decisions. "Grapho-diagnosis" is used by some physicians to detect ailments such as heart problems and neurological disorders. Psychologists and psychiatrists often use handwriting to diagnose and monitor emotional illness. Vocational interest and aptitude can often be determined by writing samples gathered by counselors.

Handwriting analyst Nadya Olyanova encourages people young and old to take handwriting analysis seriously—and to begin trying it for themselves. In an interview from her home in New York, she gave this advice: "Handwriting analysis is an index of a person's strengths and weaknesses, and through it, one can learn to help others, to encourage them and avoid hurting their feelings."

Becoming a handwriting expert—much less a graphologist—takes years. But you can enjoy some of the fun and satisfaction of the professional analyst. Learn how to interpret a few key characteristics that graphologists find most telling, and you're on your way. Place a writing sample in front of you (maybe even one of your own), and examine it in terms of the features on the next pages.

GENERAL TRAITS

LETTER BOLDNESS How thick are the letters in your sample? Even a person's decision about pen tips may give you valuable information. If you were selecting a ballpoint pen in a department store, would you choose a fine, medium, or heavy point? Do you like felt markers that produce narrow lines or wide ones?

If the strokes are thick (almost smudgy), the writer is producing **bold letters**. This kind of stroke belongs to a person who is very physically active, adventurous, and impulsive. **Average letters** are most often used by those who have a balanced interest in both money and people. **Light letters** suggest a person who is extremely sensitive, possibly somewhat timid.

SLANT Graphologists usually suggest using a chart to help with the analysis of slant.

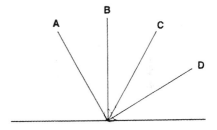

The direction in which letters lean indicates something about a person's social and emotional tendencies. Place your sample over the diagram so that the base of such ascending letters as *d*, *l*, and *b* lines up with the horizontal baseline. Then see which angle line the top of such letters most nearly and frequently touches.

A **moderate forward slant** (C) indicates the person is a healthy extrovert who feels comfortable expressing emotion and being part of a group. An **extreme forward slant** (D), however, is a sign of a person who is overly emotional, often making other people feel almost embarrassed in his or her presence. A **mild backward slant** (A) would hint at slight introversion and

143

emotional reserve. This person is probably more private than the individual whose letters lean forward. **Perpendicular writing** (B) belongs to the person who values and exhibits emotional control.

WARNING: Many handwriting experts urge extreme caution when analyzing the left slant. Peggy Mann points out in her book *The Telltale Line* (Macmillan) that left-handed people may write with a backward slant for the simple reason that it's easier. If this is the case, she advises ignoring this feature. Also, she finds this trait much less significant among younger people than among older adults. "In a middle-aged adult, letters that slant backward indicate an introvert, someone who keeps to himself or herself. However, if the subject is a preteen or teenager, a backward slant can mean a quite normal 'I won't' attitude, a breaking away from childhood patterns—someone who is trying to find his or her 'real' self."

CONNECTIONS Look at the way the letters in each word in your sample are joined or separated. **Joined letters** generally suggest a logical mind; **separated letters** an insightful one (see the sample below). Olyanova calls handwriting that is almost entirely broken up an "intuitive hand."

SIZE Look at the rectangles below. Which one best houses the majority of the letters in your handwriting?

| A |
| B |
| C |
| D |

Letter size indicates whether someone is a thinker or a doer, an introvert or an extrovert. **Small writing** (A) reflects a modest, possibly introverted nature but one characterized also by a high degree of intelligence. **Medium writing** (B) is the mark of someone who can be both private and social. **Large writing** (C) belongs to the extrovert, the confident, assured individual.

But watch out for very large script! The person with **very large writing** (D) may be showing off. It would not be surprising to learn that he or she is either vain and self-centered or desperately seeking much-needed attention.

Gerald Killbob made himself more than a nuisance in other classes, too. In science, when they were studying whales and the teacher talked about blubber, Gerald laughed out loud and said Bob must be related to whales.

She says, "Breaks in handwriting show intuition. Here, the hand unconsciously lifts itself from the paper to allow a flash of intuition to enter; and 'intuitive' hand is therefore an inspirational one." Olyanova has found that many dancers, artists, and poets write this way. When writing displays both frequent connections and frequent breaks, you can infer that the person is probably both logical and creatively intuitive.

ROUNDNESS OR SHARPNESS Are the letters smooth and round? If so, the person probably is gentle and easygoing. Do you find, instead, many sharp lines and pointed arches on the *m*'s and *n*'s? That person is displaying signs of tension and inflexibility—maybe even a stubborn streak.

LINE SLOPE Write a sample on a blank sheet of paper. Sentences will either be straight, or they will rise or fall. Graphologists find this feature an excellent indicator of your mood. As your mood changes, you may find the slope of your lines also changes. Use this chart to help you measure line slope:

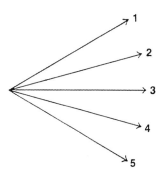

Place line 3 in a perfect 90-degree angle to the left edge of the paper your sample appears on. Then determine on which line the sentences of your sample most nearly rest.

Upward lines (2) suggest optimism, ambition, and happiness. Yet, severely upward lines (1) point to unrealistic ambition and an unhealthy desire for power. **Perfectly horizontal lines** (those close to 3) indicate a generally well-adjusted individual. **Downward lines** (4) usually belong to the pessimist or to the person who's experiencing some temporary disappointment or failure. **Severely downward lines** (5) might indicate extreme unhappiness. Olyanova says, "It could mean severe depression or skepticism. The person may even be unstable."

Harry O. Teltscher, the author of *Handwriting—Revelation of Self* (Hawthorn Books), and other experts have been fascinated by the signature of Napoleon Bonaparte. In his early signatures, there are signs of ambition and hope, as indicated by the rise of the line. Look at this signature from 1793:

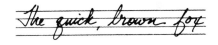

In 1805, after the battle of Austerlitz, his signature shows signs of his proud conquest.

But as setbacks occurred and his mental state deteriorated, Napoleon's signature began to slope downward more and more. His signature while living on Saint Helena, after the disastrous Waterloo campaign, was almost completely vertical, the letters practically piled one on top of the other.

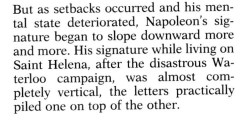

ZONES Make your own chart for zones based on the predominant height of the middle-zone letters (such as *c, a, n,* and *o*) in your sample. Draw a horizontal line along the tops and bottoms of these letters.

Next, measure the distance between the two lines, and draw two lines of identical width—one above and one below.

If the tops and bottoms of letters such as *h* and *y* fill about the same space as the middle part of the letters, the person is mature and realistic.

THE WRITING ON THE WALL

Eminent psychiatrist Alfred Adler, the "father of individual psychology," once said Nadya Olyanova "is to the science of graphology what Michelangelo is to art." So who could better analyze three writing samples from current high school students? Before reading Olyanova's analyses, draw your own conclusions about the samples. How close are you to being an expert?

145

HUMBLE The small *i* instead of a capital throughout this specimen reveals an inordinate amount of humility. She is a generous, curious person, often tenacious, as shown in the final stroke of her name. Even here, the pen is loath to leave the paper! She is intelligent, talented, trustworthy, and has a retentive memory. Her compulsiveness goes with her desire for accomplishment. She can be exacting with herself as well as with others.

well, there is only one person, actually two, whom i'd like to "get to know better." i'm sure you've figured out one of them is. i'll have to keep you in suspense and not tell you the other one. i'll talk to you soon - as soon as i have some free time (ha-ha).

love,
angella

EXECUTIVE As a child, he was given responsibilities as well as privileges and developed executive and organizational abilities. He is constructive in his thinking and has the ability to come down to essentials (shown in the single downstroke of the capital *I*). He is sensitive and friendly but does not permit a ready intimacy. Notice how each word is surrounded by lots of space. His t-bars are weak, showing a lack of self-confidence. Although logical in most of his reasoning, occasional breaks, as in the word "direction," reveal intuition.

After about five minutes I heard loud shouting coming from that direction, so I strapped on my nightstick and headed over.

MATERNAL She is sensitive, yet capable of very intense feeling, intelligent, and logical in her thinking (this is shown in the connected letters in her words, a reflection of connected thoughts). Because of a maternal instinct, she is protective in her attitude toward those weaker than herself. This is shown by the old-fashioned capital letters—the *A*, for example. Her writing, slanting to the right, tells us she is outgoing and has a need for human companionship. She is orderly, dependable, and has a retentive memory.

Dear Ann,

Hi! School is in full swing now and I'm finally settling into the rythmn of my class schedule. I'm a little scared that I've taken on too much. (I have so much homework!)

Handwriting analysis can be fun. It can also provide you with one way to know yourself, your parents and teachers, and your friends a little better. The next time someone hands you a note, check it against the handwriting features on this chart (and those discussed in the article). You may discover something no one else knows.

Feature	Sample	Trait
Bold letters	*quite a*	ACTIVE, DARING, IMPULSIVE, SENSUOUS
Average-size letters	*will you please*	WELL-BALANCED, DIVERSE
Light letters	*how much*	SENSITIVE, PERCEPTIVE
Very large writing	*Cinema*	ATTENTION-SEEKING, SHOWY
Large writing	*future*	EXTROVERTED, SOCIAL, ENTHUSIASTIC
Medium-size writing	*type of analysis*	ACTIVE, CONTEMPLATIVE
Small writing	*from everywhere and from Toronto*	INTROVERTED, ANALYTICAL
Large spaces between words	*I would be very interested*	ALOOF, MISTRUSTFUL
Small spaces between words	*almost impossible for me*	NARROW-MINDED, RIGID
Large capitals	*Maybe that's the only*	PROUD, EGOTISTICAL
Small capitals	*Whenever*	MODEST, HUMBLE
Final stroke upward	*had always filled*	SOCIAL, GRACIOUS, FRIENDLY, ARTISTIC
Final stroke downward	*Sincerely yours*	AGGRESSIVE, UNFRIENDLY
Final stroke horizontal	*the other + young son*	GENEROUS, CURIOUS
Legible	*I am quite interested*	COMMUNICATIVE
Illegible	*not LT me eat. Being*	UNCOMMUNICATIVE, PRIVATE, NERVOUS
Frequent underscoring	*You are the best*	FANATIC, EMPHATIC

t-bar:		i-dot:	
Detached, to right	PRODUCTIVE, ENERGETIC	**High above letter**	IMAGINATIVE
Detached, to left	LAZY, UNPRODUCTIVE	**To right of letter**	OPTIMISTIC, ENTHUSIASTIC
Slanted downward	AGGRESSIVE, DEFENSIVE	**Directly above letter**	CAREFUL, PRECISE
Lifted above stem	IMAGINATIVE, SPIRITUAL	**Heavy and above letter**	AGGRESSIVE, UNKIND
Straight across stem	DISCIPLINED, CONFIDENT	**Very light**	DEPENDENT, TIMID
Starlike, over stem	PERSISTENT, DILIGENT	**To left of letter**	CAUTIOUS, FEARFUL
Starlike, short of stem	HESITANT	**Circled**	ARTISTIC, PRETENTIOUS

If the **top zone** letters are especially high, reaching beyond the top line, the person has ideals, dreams, ambitions, and (quite literally) "high" hopes. The strokes indicate the tendency to reach up and strive.

Bottom zone letters that extend beyond the lower boundary line usually point to physical or emotional excesses. Olyanova interprets them this way: "Essentially, this shows a measure of confusion, where the emotions heat up the brain and impair judgment. But it can also mean a sense of the dramatic, a flair for the unusual.

If the upper- and lower-zone letters hover close to the **middle zone,** without especially high or low loops, you can make a safe guess that the person is very practical.

SPECIFIC TRAITS

Now look at a few **specific traits** of your handwriting sample for further information about personality.

T-BARS You probably have never looked closely at the different ways people cross their *t's*. But the t-bar gives the graphologist one of his or her most valuable clues.

A   B   C   D   E

The bar that spins away from the stem toward the right (A) is a much more positive formation than the one that spins toward the left (B). Toward the right, the disconnected bar shows eagerness and willingness to finish projects. Toward the left, the bar indicates a tendency to put things off and to be indecisive and weak-willed.

Look at sample C. At times, you will meet someone who is very much afraid of criticism and becomes immediately defensive when he or she is corrected. It would not be surprising to find this kind of t-bar from such a person. Both the defensiveness and the aggression that sometimes accompanies it are suggested by the hard downward stroke.

The lifting of the t-bar in sample D is not unlike the rise already discussed for other letters. This cross is produced by a person with imagination and dreams. Sample E shows good control:

The t-bar crosses through the stem and is balanced on either side of it.

I-DOTS The dot above the lowercase *i* is another feature you may not have paid attention to before. A typewriter always places the dot neatly above the letter. Look at the *i's* on this page. Now look at the *i's* in your sample.

Do you find *i's* with the dots high above the letter? This person has a good and active imagination. If the dot is high and to the right, the person is very positive about most things and breeds enthusiasm in others. Dots that look typewritten, appearing directly above the letter in approximately the same boldness as the letter, suggest a careful, persistent, hardworking nature.

But watch out for some dots! A heavy dot may indicate an authoritarian personality, someone who likes to boss others around. A very light dot belongs to the follower and the timid soul. A dot that appears far off to the left will be found in the handwriting of people who seldom complete tasks and are overly cautious. Omitting dots altogether sends the message of carelessness or forgetfulness.

There's one dot that must be interpreted with special care: the circle dot. It may indicate either a desire to be different and get attention or a genuine artistic flair.

WARNING: The different possible interpretations for the circle dot should make you aware of another important feature of handwriting analysis. Be sure you look at specific traits that have a range of interpretations *in light of your other conclusions.* If there are other signs of attention-seeking in a person's script, you should read the circle dot as just another exaggeration. But if a person's script is genuinely and consistently artistic, you should see the circle dot as an additional sign of the artist.

CAPITALS Capitals are diagnosed largely the same way as general letter size. Very large capitals are usually written by people with big egos. Small capitals often belong to the more modest and timid. But loops, closures, and decoration give hints as important as size.

Olyanova finds a few capitals especially interesting. Look at these two *F's:*

The first, she calls "vulgar and uneducated." But the second, less dressy and more direct, almost printlike, she labels "constructive."

As you look at these various handwriting features, jot down those that are important and prominent in your particular sample. Gradually watch a portrait as real as a photograph develop right before your eyes. Then write a paragraph in which you summarize your findings. Be sure to mention any contradictions. Few people are completely consistent and predictable.

Use your new knowledge to understand yourself and other people. That's what graphology is all about. And that's what Olyanova means when she tells us that the most important function of graphology is "to help us become more tolerant and loving."

Source: Joyce Dyer, "Analyze Your Handwriting (and Everyone Else's!)," *Seventeen Magazine,* January 1986, p. 93. Reprinted by permission of Joyce Dyer.

DISCUSSING YOUR IDEAS

When you have finished, discuss your ideas in class. Your teacher may ask you how you feel about graphoanalysis and whether what you have discovered about another person through graphoanalysis seems plausible.

Organizing the Mini Research Paper

Now that you have gathered your information and discussed it, use the *organizational matrix* on page 150 to develop your ideas and to guide your writing. Develop your *thesis sentence* and then list the *main ideas* you will use to support it.

Draw examples, reasons, and details from the articles to support them. To do this, sort your note cards and arrange them by *main idea.* Write these entries in the column marked *Citations.* Eliminate any cards that do not support your thesis.

When you have arranged your information on the matrix, think of a lively *attention-getting sentence.* Combine your *main ideas* into a concise *sentence of method.* These sentences, along with your *thesis statement,* will make up the introduction to your mini research paper.

Enter this information on the *organizational matrix.* When you are ready to write, use the matrix to assemble your mini research paper. Generally, each *main idea* unit will become a *body paragraph.* Make certain each begins with a strong *topic sentence.* The *body sentences* will come from the main ideas and details, supported by the citations. End your essay with a *concluding paragraph* which sums up your information and finishes with a *closer sentence.*

Before you begin writing your mini research paper, read the next section on how to incorporate quoted material into a document. Then use it as a reference so that you can make smooth transitions from your writing to the quotes taken from your sources.

Use this organizational matrix to guide the development of your mini research paper.

Topic: _____

Thesis Statement: _____

_____

**Sentence of
Method:** _____

_____

Attention-getting Sentence: _____

_____

MAIN IDEAS	SUPPORTING DETAILS	CITATIONS

MAIN IDEAS	SUPPORTING DETAILS	CITATIONS

Using Your Notes To Cite Quotations

Once you have organized your information, you need to incorporate quotes and other notes into your document. In this text, we are using the MLA rules of style for parenthetical footnotes. This means that when you use material from one of your sources, you will place in parentheses the author's last name and the page number the material comes from.

Example:

> "Several market observers said that when institutional investors do well, individuals benefit from those gains" (Ebersole 100).

It is important to note that quotation marks go before and after the exact words copied. The end quotation mark is followed by a parenthesis, the author's last name, and the page number. Close the parentheses and add a period. The period goes after the citation, not after the quote.

In addition to quotation marks ("), there are single quotation marks ('). These are used when a writer quotes someone who is quoting someone else. For example, suppose a writer wishes to use a quote by Jeff Schaeffer which appeared in the article "Health Is Contagious." If you want to use Jeff Schaeffer's words in your writing, you must write:

> " 'People confuse trading with ownership' " (Ebersole quoting Schaeffer 10D).

NOW YOU DO IT

1. Find a line in Robert Frost's poem which you like and quote it. (See pages 49–50.)
2. Find a quotation in a newspaper or magazine article and write it as a quote within a quote. Be sure to include the citation.

Writing Quotes

The main rule to remember is to use quotes *when you use the exact words of a writer or speaker*. Next, you need to know the rules for using quotation marks with other marks of punctuation. These are as follows:

1. Put periods and commas *inside* the quotation marks except when you include a citation.

Example:

> "Whether you like it or not," he said, "the research paper will be due Friday."
>
> Dr. Melon said, "Beginning Wednesday, all freshmen will have to pay the student activity fee at the beginning of each term."

Exception:

> "The definition of plagiarism simply means that an author's words and ideas are his property and anyone who borrows those words or ideas must acknowledge her source" (Barlow 199).

Notice that the period goes *after* the page number that the quote was taken from, but the quotation marks go *after the last word of the quote*.

2. Write commas that follow quoted material within the quotation marks.

Example:

> "Writing a research paper can be a very rewarding experience," my English teacher told us.
>
> "This is true," she said, "particularly if you uncover some new information."

3. If you use a colon (:) or semicolon(;), place it outside the quotation marks.

Example:

> He said the following: "Everyone will report to the playing field at 6 a.m. sharp!"

4. Place a dash, a question mark, or an exclamation point inside the quotation mark *when it goes with quoted material*. Place it outside the quotation marks when it belongs to the sentence that the quoted material is in.

Example:

> He asked, "Where did this come from?"

What does the expression "chill out" mean?

They jeered, "Throw the umpire out!"

How can you say, "Throw the umpire out"?

5. Following quoted material, enclose within parentheses the name of the author and the page number of the book the material comes from.

Example:

"A common indicator of the mental health of a country is reflected in the toys children play with" (Lawler 45).

Notice that the period comes *after* the parentheses.

6. If the material you quote is something that someone else has said, we call that a quote within a quote and use both double and single quotation marks to indicate this.

Example:

Susan said, "My favorite poem begins with 'Whose woods these are I think I know/His house is in the village though.'"

Notice that we use two sets of quotation marks, one to show what Susan has said (which is the entire sentence) and one to show that she is quoting what the poet Robert Frost wrote.

7. Quotes that are longer than *three* lines should be indented with a larger margin on each side and single spaced. This is called *block quoting*. Skip two lines between the text and the quoted material. Do *not* use quotation marks around *block quoted* material. It should look like this:

This is important to the teacher of ESOL who must determine how to teach a student whose cultural experience has taught him, for example, that a

text [is] . . . a fixed unit in which everything is of equal importance. Text is so to speak a plateau rather than a hierarchical structure of statements. Such a perception becomes quite evident if one looks at the physical aspects of the Koran, which, as is well known, does not have any paragraphs. . . .Since the reader is expected to impress upon his mind such records even if he does not understand what has been written, nearly the only way to handle such a text is to memorize and recite it (Osterloh in Valdes 78–79).

This method of learning is in direct contrast to methods used in the United States.

Incorporating Quoted Material into Your Document

It is important to incorporate quoted material into the text in a natural way. This can be achieved by using introductory expressions.

Examples:

> As Professor _____ noted, "_____" (   ).
>
> As shown by _____ "_____" (   ).
>
> George M. Genzel said, "_____" (   ).
>
> As demonstrated in Martha G. Miller's work,
> "_____" (   ).
>
> Dr. _____ supports this when he says, "_____" (   ).
>
> Professor _____ contradicts this idea by "_____" (   ).

There are many ways to incorporate material, but one of the most effective is to use the quoted material to complete your sentence:

> Such jokes fit well the notion that much humor veils aggression, permitting the joke teller, in Freud's words, "to be malicious with dignity" (Freud 102).

USING ELLIPSES

When using quoted material, you may find that the quote is too long. Sometimes you like the beginning of the material and need to include words at the end. If this is the case, you may omit the words you do not want to use as long as you replace them with an ellipsis mark. An ellipsis mark consists of three dots (. . .) that show that a word or group of words have been omitted. If you omit a sentence or sentences, then you must use four dots (. . . .) instead of three to show that you have omitted a sentence. Of course, ellipsis marks may not be used to change the meaning of the original.

Look at the material below. Note how the ellipsis is used to eliminate material the author did not wish to include. When using ellipsis marks, it is important to make certain the resulting product is grammatically correct and logical. It is not necessary to use ellipsis marks before or after quoted words that are obviously part of a sentence.

Original Quote:

> "Both Mr. Morin and Mrs. Kurtz noted that the best strategy to use during a job interview is honesty. The interviewee should provide a comprehensive description of his employment record and responsibilities. This should be combined with tact in that the prospective candidate should concentrate on his accomplishments and contribution to

his employer rather than spend time telling what is wrong with his boss."

Using Ellipsis Marks:

"Both Mr. Morin and Mrs. Kurtz noted that the best strategy to use during a job interview is honesty. . . . This should be combined with tact in that the prospective candidate should concentrate on his accomplishments . . . rather than spend time telling what is wrong with his boss."

USING BRACKETS

Another important tool for using quoted material is brackets [ ]. Brackets are used to change or insert a word to make the quote clearer or to make it fit the sentence you are inserting it into. You can use brackets in the middle of your quotation if you need to explain something, to clarify a statement, or to correct something the person said.

"Both Mr. Morin and Mrs. Kurtz noted that the best strateg[ies] to use during a job interview are honesty . . . . [and] tact."

USING "SIC"

If there is an error in the original, such as a typographical or grammatical error, you may use the word "sic" to indicate that you did not make the spelling or other error but rather that it appeared as you are quoting it. Consider this example:

Thru [sic] careful study, the researchers noted that people are more likely to purchase garden fertilizer packaged in green.

In this case, the word "sic" indicates that the word "thru" is misspelled in the text and that this is not the writer's error. ("Sic" comes from Latin and means thus, so.) Notice line 5, page 130 in "Chinese Characters in Computers."

Sample Research Paper

Before you begin the mini research paper, let's examine a short section of a master's thesis which uses the techniques we have discussed in this chapter. Please read it carefully and then answer the questions which follow.

THE RATIONALE BEHIND THIS STUDY AND ITS RELATIONSHIP
TO ESOL

1. The cultural backgrounds of others are of special concern to the
2. communicator because "each listener has internalized to some
3. extent the critical standards of his or her cultural heritage" (Ried
4. 1979, 63).

5. In the ESOL classroom in the United States, student
6. representatives of many cultures gather to communicate in the
7. medium of English. Communication for them is dependent on how
8. well they can use their newly learned language. Their acquisition
9. of language, i.e., internalization and ability to use the language as
10. distinguished from learning the rules that govern the language,
11. is, according to recent studies, dependent upon three factors.
12. These factors are the filter, the organizer, and the monitor.
   (Krashen 45).

13. Language learners do not take in everything they hear. Their
14. motives, needs, attitudes, and emotional states filter what
15. they hear, and therefore affect the rate and quality of
16. language learning. We use the term 'filter' to refer to these
17. 'affective' factors that screen out certain parts of learners'
18. language environments.

19. The organizer is that part of a language learner's mind
20. which works subconsciously to organize the new language
21. system. It gradually builds up the rule system of the new
22. language . . . and is used by the learner to generate
23. sentences not learned through memorization.

24. The monitor is that part of the learner's internal system that
25. consciously processes information. When the learner
26. memorizes grammar rules and tries to apply them
27. consciously during conversation, for example, we say the
28. person is relying on the monitor (Krashen 46).

29. Since teaching ESOL, by its very nature, implies that people from
30. different language and cultural backgrounds learn a new
31. language, the question arises as to whether different cultures
32. affect the filter and people's "motives, needs, attitudes, and
33. emotional states," (Reid, 1987 87). Joy Reid, of Colorado State
34. University, developed a questionnaire in which she had 1,388
35. students identify their perceptual learning styles. The results of
36. her study

37. indicated that NNS's [nonnative speakers] learning
38. style preferences often differ significantly from those of NS;
39. that ESL students from different language backgrounds
40. sometimes differ from one another in their learning style
41. preferences (Reid 1987, 87).

42 Among the questions she poses as a result of this self-reported
43 questionnaire are: "(a) how to 'match' students' learning style
44 preferences with 'teacher styles' and (b) whether or not student
45 learning style preferences are malleable" (Reid 1987, 99).

46 Reid's work investigates perceptual learning styles: visual,
47 auditory, and kinesthetic. Reid concludes from her study "the
48 relationship between teaching and learning styles and
49 developmental processes also need to be studied (1987, 103). She
50 questions whether "beginning language learners [should] be
51 taught initially in their preferred learning styles in order to
52 reduce what Krashen calls the affective filter" (103).

53 Increased attention seems to be focused on learning preferences.
54 At the 1987 TESOL Convention in Miami Beach, Florida, Linda
55 Tobash and Marian Blaber presented their findings of student
56 perceptions of teachers and how those perceptions match the
57 perceptions of their students. Among dissatisfied learners, the
58 Chinese were second most dissatisfied, followed by the Spanish
59 speakers. Students' perceptions of what a classroom or what
60 instruction should be like were not being met.

61 Madeline Ehrman, in an unpublished paper prepared for the
62 Foreign Service Institute, used the MBTI to investigate the
63 personality styles of nonnative speakers of English who were
64 teaching their native language to American U.S. government
65 employees and their spouses (Ehrman and Oxford 1987).

66 This thesis adds to the limited body of research on personality
67 styles of nonnative speakers by investigating personality style;
68 introversion and extraversion; sensing and intuition; judging and
69 perceiving; thinking and feeling of students in ESOL programs
70 and of teachers of ESOL. It asks what effect a person's culture has
71 on how he or she prefers to learn and it provides data on which
72 personality preferences are preferred by people from different
73 cultural backgrounds.

BIBLIOGRAPHY

Allen, Virginia French, *Inside English*. New York: Regents Publishing Co., 1983.

Blaber, Marian, and Linda Tobash, "ESL Faculty Perceptions of Students' Needs," paper presented at TESOL, Miami Beach, Florida, 1987.

Brislin, Richard, ed., *Culture Learning: Concepts, Applications, and Research*. An East-West Center Book, University of Hawaii, 1977.

Dulay, Heidi, Marina Burt, and Stephen Krashen, *Language 2*. New York: Oxford University Press, 1982.

Genzel, Rhona, and Martha Graves Cummings. *Culturally Speaking*. New York: Harper & Row, 1986.

Hoffman, Jeffrey L., and Marianne Betkouski. "A Summary of Myers-Briggs Type Indicator Research Applications in Education." *Research in Psychological Type*, vol. 3, 1981.

Krashen, Stephen D., and Tracy D. Terrell. *The Natural Approach*. San Francisco: Alemany Press, 1983.

Myers, I. B., *Introduction to Type*, Palo Alto, Calif.: Consulting Psychologists Press, 1962.

Myers, I. B., *The Myers-Briggs Type Indicator: Manual*. Palo Alto, Calif.: Consulting Psychologists Press, 1962.

Myers, I. B., and P. B. Myers, *Gifts Differing*. Palo Alto, Calif.: Consulting Psychologists Press, 1980.

Reid, Joy M., "The Learning Style Preference of ESL Students." *TESOL Quarterly* 21, no. 1(1987):87-103.

NOW YOU DO IT

After reading the segment from the master's thesis, answer the following questions:

1. On page 156, line 3, who is Ried? What does 1979 tell you? What does 63 tell you?
2. Why is a large segment on the first page indented?
3. What do the three dots on page 156, line 22, tell the reader?
4. Why do 'match' and 'teaching styles' have single quotes? (Lines 43 and 44.) How do you think they appeared in the original?
5. Why are brackets around the word 'should' on page 157, line 50?
6. Why is the number (103) placed in parentheses? (Page 157, line 52.) Why is more information provided in other citations?
7. What is the title of Krashen's book (line 28) and who published it?
8. Where was Reid's (line 33) work published? What was the title of her article?
9. Why do you suppose 1987 appears in lines 33, 41, and 45? (Hint: The bibliography is not complete.)
10. Notice that line 12 has a citation that refers you to page 45 in Krashen. The material is not a quote. Why is there a citation? (Hint: See the article on plagiarism where it discusses Molly. Also refer to page 119, #4.)
11. Why are no ellipsis marks used in lines 2, 32, or 37?

Writing the Mini Research Paper

Now you are ready to write your mini research paper. Using your organizational matrix and information you have gathered reading the two articles on graphoanalysis write an essay on the subject in which you analyze your classmate's handwriting. Be sure to include quotes, to provide citations for paraphrased material, and to use ellipsis marks, brackets, and parenthetical footnotes, when they apply.

Ten
The Research Project

Some students drop college classes or decide not to register for elective courses because they require a research project. After completing this chapter, however, you will not find research papers so intimidating. In fact, you will be prepared to tackle them with confidence and enthusiasm.

In this section, you will go through the steps of writing a research paper, including:

☐ Choosing a topic
☐ Narrowing the topic
☐ Doing library research
☐ Writing a bibliography and note cards
☐ Developing outlines
☐ Participating in a debate
☐ Writing a research paper

You are probably surprised to learn that you will be participating in a debate as part of your research-paper project. If you are like most students, you have found that presenting your findings in an organized way is far more difficult than doing the research. Participating in a debate will help you organize your information for an audience. It will also allow you to get feedback from your audience so that you will know where the strengths and weaknesses of your arguments are. Then, if necessary, you can do additional research or reorganize your information before writing your paper.

Choosing a Topic

Choosing your topic for investigation is crucial. First, select a topic which interests you. You are going to be spending a great deal of time researching, debating, and presenting your topic in a research paper.

Second, make sure your topic is researchable by doing preliminary research. This means that after you identify a topic you are interested in, you go to the library to clarify and to narrow your topic. This preliminary research will often help you find an even more interesting aspect of a topic you had not thought of before. It will also tell you if research material is available on a topic.

Third, choose a topic that can be proven through the use of facts. Do not choose a topic that is based primarily on emotional or religious issues.

Examples of topics you may wish to investigate are:

1. Is the quarter system more advantageous to students than the semester system?
2. Should employers be required to provide child care for their employees' children?
3. Should governments use capital punishment?
4. Should the United States continue to fund the NASA space program?
5. Should countries discontinue building and licensing nuclear power plants?

NOW YOU DO IT

Think of some topics you are interested in researching. List them below.

1. _____
2. _____
3. _____
4. _____
5. _____

Share your list with your classmates and develop a large list of topics. Once this has been done, look over the list and decide which topics interest you. You may choose as many as you like at first. After you make your decision, your instructor will count the number of students interested in each topic and eliminate those which few people are interested in.

The next step is the final topic selection. Your instructor will ask you to indicate which topic you are most interested in researching. Four people may select the same topic. These four people will become a *debate team*. Two individuals will present the *affirmative side* (in favor of the topic) and two individuals will present the *negative side* (against the topic).

Preparing for the Debate

WRITING THE DEBATE PROPOSITION

Once everyone has chosen a topic and has been assigned to a *debate team*, the *debate team* must restate the topic as a *proposition*. Writing a strong proposition is vital because it will shape your debate, delineate your argument, and indicate your areas for research.

The *proposition* is a statement which has the following properties:

☐ It can be supported through research. This allows the argument to be made on logic and evidence rather than opinion.

Example:

> Smoking marijuana is morally wrong. (incorrect—deals with moral judgments rather than facts)
>
> Smoking marijuana can cause chromosome damage, lead to use of stronger drugs, and result in decreased productivity. (correct)

☐ It is worded as a declarative sentence rather than as a question or a phrase. This allows the participants to choose a side and indicates the role of the negative and the affirmative teams.

Example:

> Should credit-card interest be frozen at 16 percent? (incorrect—worded in question form)
>
> Credit card interest: ripoff or merchants' right? (incorrect—worded as a phrase)
>
> Credit card interest should be frozen at 16 percent to avoid windfall profits by credit companies at the expense of unwary consumers. (correct)

☐ It is worded in a positive manner. (Do not use *negatives* like *not, no, never.*) Positive wording encourages direct rather than negative arguments.

Example:

> Employers should *not* be required to provide child care for employees' children. (incorrect)
>
> Employers *should* be required to provide child care for employees' children. (correct)

☐ It contains *specific wording* that is agreed upon in advance by both teams. If both sides don't agree on the wording, the teams will end up debating the meaning of words rather than the merits of the proposition.

Example:

> Capital punishment is *wrong.* (incorrect—"wrong" is not specific enough. People have differing ideas of right and wrong.)
>
> Capital punishment is unconstitutional because poor or minority prisoners are sentenced to death more frequently than are white or wealthy prisoners who commit similar offenses. (correct)

□ It contains no general or all-inclusive phrases (e.g., *all, every, always*). There is an exception to any proposition worded with *all, every,* or *always.* An opposing debater can find that exception and use it to negate the team's argument.

Example:

Everyone should have to work for a living rather than receive welfare from the government. (incorrect. What about small children or those who are gravely ill and unable to work?)

Individuals who are physically able to work should be required to perform some needed job in order to receive government assistance. (correct—"individuals" is defined)

□ It is worded opposite to the *status quo*, the situation that exists presently. Rather than debating an existing situation, word the proposition to reflect a change.

Example:

A pregnant woman should be allowed to have an abortion during the first trimester of her pregnancy. (incorrect. This is the law in the United States.)

A pregnant woman should be allowed to have an abortion only until the eighth week of pregnancy. (correct. Sets limits and is different from the current law.)

□ It is fresh, interesting, and thought-provoking.

Examples:

Speed limits should be eliminated on U.S. highways.

Free trade should exist between ＿＿＿＿＿ and ＿＿＿＿＿.
             country   country

NOW YOU DO IT

Before you try to develop a *debate proposition* with your team, reword each of the five topics you developed on page 162 as a debate proposition. Have your instructor check your work before you continue.

1. ＿＿＿＿＿＿＿＿＿＿＿＿＿＿＿＿＿＿＿＿＿＿＿＿＿＿＿＿＿＿＿＿

2. ＿＿＿＿＿＿＿＿＿＿＿＿＿＿＿＿＿＿＿＿＿＿＿＿＿＿＿＿＿＿＿＿

3. ＿＿＿＿＿＿＿＿＿＿＿＿＿＿＿＿＿＿＿＿＿＿＿＿＿＿＿＿＿＿＿＿

4. ＿＿＿＿＿＿＿＿＿＿＿＿＿＿＿＿＿＿＿＿＿＿＿＿＿＿＿＿＿＿＿＿

5. ＿＿＿＿＿＿＿＿＿＿＿＿＿＿＿＿＿＿＿＿＿＿＿＿＿＿＿＿＿＿＿＿

Now, *with your debate team*, write a debate proposition from a topic you have chosen. Have your instructor approve your proposition before you continue.

_____

_____

_____

DETERMINING DEBATE-TEAM SIDES

The next step is to decide who will represent each side in your debate. There are two sides: the *affirmative team*, which is *for* the proposition, and the *negative team*, which is *against* the proposition. In the space below, write the names of the two members of each team:

Affirmative Team   **Negative Team**

_____   _____

_____   _____

DEBATE-TEAM RESPONSIBILITIES

The word *"team,"* from now on, refers to the two individuals who are debating a particular side of the proposition. They have the following responsibilities:

1. To do research independently of each other.
2. To meet to compare notes and to determine who will speak first in the debate.
3. To determine the most effective order for presenting debate information.
4. To work together to develop three matrices: offensive, defensive, and attack strategy. These will be discussed in detail on page 167–173.
5. To prepare two visual aids (charts, graphs, transparencies, slides, handouts, photographs, etc.) to use during the debate.

Doing Library Research

A debate or research paper is based on facts, data, and other information gathered through systematic investigation. Besides library research, research may also include studies you have done yourself. For example, you could report on the results of an experiment or a survey you have conducted.

When doing library research, you should do the following:

1. If you are unfamiliar with the library you will be using, ask the librarian if the library offers tours. If it does, take a tour of the library.
2. Learn how the information in the library is made available. Is information listed in a card catalogue or has it been computerized? If you don't know how to use the system, ask the librarian.
3. Familiarize yourself with the microfiche and microfilm collections. Learn how to access articles with this system.
4. Find out if there is an interlibrary loan system so that you can obtain books and materials that are not at your library but are available at other libraries. Often universities cooperate by making their libraries accessible to students from other colleges.
5. Learn how to use the *Reader's Guide to Periodical Literature*.
6. Discover where journals in your area of interest are located.
7. Find out if your library has a *copier card system*. If it does, you can buy a card and then use it instead of coins to make photocopies of material that you wish to take with you. Learn how this system works.
8. Find out where the copiers are, how to use them, and how much they cost to use per page.
9. Learn how the library is organized so that you know where to look for material.
10. Write down the hours the library is open.

Once you are familiar with the library and know where things are, use the catalogue or computer system to identify materials on your topic. Remember that information can usually be found under three headings: *subject, title,* and *author.* You will probably begin your search by looking up your topic under the *subject* heading. For example, if you are searching for information on nuclear power plants, you would look in the *subject heading* under *"nuclear power plants"* or *"nuclear power."*

As you identify your sources, *write them down carefully* on your *bibliography cards.* Record *all* the information and check it carefully. Few things are more annoying than having to make a second trip to the library to locate a source that you wrote down incompletely or incorrectly!

EXAMINING SOURCES

Once you locate your source, you are ready to examine it carefully. First, check the book's *table of contents* and *index* or scan the article to determine whether it is relevant to your topic. Many sources, although they look promising in the catalogue or index, will not be useful and should be discarded. However, if the material is relevant to your topic, either read it at the library and take notes or check it out and read it at home. If the source is an article, you may wish to copy it for later reference.

Follow the procedures in Chapter 8 for preparing bibliography and note cards. Your instructor will ask you to hand in your bibliography and note-cards so that he or she can check them as you proceed through your research project.

Preparing a Debate Matrix

When you have completed your research, meet with your debate partner. Together you will share information, prepare three debate organizational matrices, and develop and rehearse your team's debate strategy.

THE OFFENSIVE DEBATE MATRIX

Regardless of whether you and your partner are the *affirmative* or the *negative team*, the first step is to develop an *offensive debate matrix*. This matrix outlines the main arguments you will use to convince your listeners to support your side of the proposition. This matrix includes the following:

1. The debate proposition
2. Main ideas which support the thesis listed in *order of importance*, with the most important ideas listed first.
3. Supporting ideas which develop the main ideas
4. Specific examples and details to illustrate supporting ideas
5. Documentation references

THE DEFENSIVE DEBATE MATRIX

It is not enough just to know how you will present your information; you must also analyze your opponent's argument and strategy. Therefore, the second step is to develop a *defensive debate matrix*. The purpose of this outline is to help you to identify weak or questionable aspects of your argument and to formulate methods to offset or defend against your opponent's attack. This matrix includes the following:

1. Any main points which you intend to use which may be open to question or which may be attacked by your opponent
2. Any points which you *do not* intend to use but which your opponent may bring up against you
3. Supporting materials and specific strategies which you will use to combat the attack

On the following page is an example of an offensive and a defensive debate matrix used in a class debate. Notice how the ideas are developed and how the writers use details and examples to support the proposition.

OFFENSIVE DEBATE MATRIX

Team: <u>Negative</u>

Proposition: <u>There Should Be Unlimited Speed on U.S. Highways.</u>

MAIN IDEAS	SUPPORTING IDEAS	DETAILS/EXAMPLES (DOCUMENTATION REFERENCES)
High speed creates more accidents.	Lower accident rates occurred after the speed was limited to 55 mph in 1974. Car accident rates went up in states which raised the rural highway speed limit to 65 mph, whereas states which kept the 55 mph experienced a decrease in accident rates. A driver has more reaction time and control when driving at slower speeds.	In 1974 when the speed was limited to 55 mph, the fatality rate in highway car accidents fell from 55,000 in 1973 to 46,000. In Arizona, after raising the interstate highway speed limit to 65 mph, there were 51 fatalities, as opposed to 19 at 55 mph, an increase of 168%.
The higher the speed, the more chance of death by accident.	Every additional 10 mph over 55 mph doubles the chance of death by car accident. The faster a car drives the greater the amount of energy it generates. Thus, fatality and severe damage occur in high-speed, high-energized car accidents. Small cars have less protection than big cars. Because of this, especially at high speeds, death by car accident can and does occur more frequently in small cars. Because smaller cars are more prevalent today, the fatality rate has increased.	A driver traveling at 75 mph has four times greater chance of death by car crash than a person driving at 55 mph. According to the laws of physics, the greater the amount of energy propelling the colliding items (cars), the worse the damage is resulting from the collision. A Yugo is less safe in a car crash than a Lincoln Continental because the car frame is smaller. If smaller cars, which have gained in popularity due to good gas mileage, drive faster than 55 mph, the car accident results are more severe.

DEFENSIVE DEBATE MATRIX

Team: Negative

Proposition: There Should Be Unlimited Speed On U.S. Highways.

MAIN IDEAS	SUPPORTING IDEAS	DETAILS/EXAMPLES (DOCUMENTATION REFERENCES)
Driving at 55 mph saves money.	Money is saved on gas because the car engine does not work as hard. Bigger-engine cars, which people would eventually buy in order to drive faster, would cost more money to produce and would use more fuel. Driving faster than 55 mph would be costly. Because accident and fatality rates would increase, insurance premiums, automotive repair, property reimbursements, and medical costs would all rise.	Of two identical cars traveling 1000 miles at different speeds, the faster-traveling car used 10 gallons of gas more than the slower-traveling car. A Porsche costs more money to produce, run, and maintain than a Subaru Justy. The U.S. insurance industry estimates car-related insurance costs at $80 billion annually. If collisions, injuries, and claims increase, so will premiums. Per capita: estimated deaths cost $240,000; nonfatal injuries cost $10,800; and property damage costs $1600.
Although highway roads are designed for speeds up to 75 mph, people and cars are not designed to withstand speeds above 55 mph.	At higher speeds, the driver has less reaction time for road conditions. Of all car accidents, death occurs most frequently in highway accidents.	According to the laws of physics, cars driving at higher speeds require more space and time to stop than slower-traveling cars. Highway car accidents comprise 18% of the annual number of U.S. car accidents. This percentage claims 52% of annual car accident fatalities.

THE ATTACK-STRATEGY MATRIX

The old Indian proverb "Love your friends but know your enemies" applies to debate in that, to win, you must analyze your opponent's strong and weak points. This requires creative thinking and analysis. To develop the two other matrices, you asked yourself, "What are my strong and weak points and what specific information can I use to convince the audience to support my side?" Now you must apply this question to your opponent's argument. This will provide the basis for your attack during the debate.

The *attack-strategy matrix* should contain the following:

1. Your opponent's strong points in *order of importance*
2. Your material and strategy to discredit them
3. Your opponent's weak points
4. Your material and strategy to capitalize on them

Don't show or discuss your material with anyone other than your partner. If you have any questions or concerns, ask your instructor.

On the following page is an example of an *attack-strategy matrix*. Notice how the writers identify weak arguments and plan to attack their opponents' arguments.

ATTACK-STRATEGY MATRIX

OPPONENTS' STRONG POINTS	ATTACK STRATEGY
Money is saved by eliminating the speed limit. 1. Fewer hours would be spent driving. This time could be used for other things.	The time saved by driving faster would not be used for work. It would be used, by most people, for themselves (T.V., shopping, sleeping, etc.). So no money is saved.
2. There would be no need for police patrol on highways. 3. There would be no need for radar detectors.	More money would be saved by preventing accidents than by eliminating highway police patrol.
	No price can be put on the desire to live or on the impact of a death.
Drivers can determine how fast they wish to drive according to what they feel is safe and good.	Not all people use good judgment. 1. For example, people drive while intoxicated. 2. Accidents are determined by more factors than a driver's judgment, such as road condition, car safety and other drivers' behavior, etc. . . . (Drivers are not perfect!)

OPPONENTS' WEAK POINTS	ATTACK STRATEGY
Unlimited speed is more convenient because it saves time and aggravation.	For all benefits there is a cost. 1. Time saved is minimal. According to research, only seven hours per speeding car per year is saved. 2. Also, accidents create traffic jams and waste time. 3. Different speeds would cause drivers aggravation. Also, the drivers will have to concentrate more on the road situation.
Most people drive at speeds higher than 55 mph despite the law. People vote with their gas pedals, i.e., the general public is in favor of higher speeds.	Recent polls show that 66% of the population is in favor of keeping the 55 mph speed limit. An example—the fact that a lot of people commit crimes does not mean that crime should be legalized.

OPPONENTS' STRONG POINTS	ATTACK STRATEGY
Assuming that more fatal and nonfatal accidents occur at higher speeds, people still drive faster than the law permits. Why create speed limits if most people break them?	Even though people drive at speeds higher than 55 mph, it is a smaller amount than those who drove above 55 mph when the speed limit was higher.

Conclusion: The reasons for maintaining the 55 mph speed limit far outweigh the arguments for changing the law.

EVALUATING THE DEBATE MATRIX

Before you go to the "Now You Do It" section, examine the examples of *offensive, defensive,* and *attack-strategy matrices* on the preceding and following pages. After you answer these questions, discuss your findings with two other students. Compare your findings and decide the weaknesses and strengths of the arguments and ways to improve them.

1. What are the primary arguments of the negative side?

   _____

   _____

   _____

   _____

2. Are the examples given by the negative side strong enough to support their argument? Why or why not?

   _____

   _____

   _____

   _____

3. Where are the weaknesses in the negative side's argument?

   _____

   _____

   _____

   _____

4. How does the negative side intend to attack the affirmative's argument? Will their strategy work? Why or why not?

   _____

   _____

   _____

   _____

5. What would you add or delete to strengthen the negative side's offensive and defensive strategies?

_____

_____

_____

_____

EXAMPLE: OFFENSIVE DEBATE MATRIX

Team: <u>Negative</u>

Proposition: <u>A Person Should Have the Right to Take His or Her Own Life if He or She is Terminally Ill.</u>

MAIN IDEAS	SUPPORTING IDEAS	DETAILS/EXAMPLES (DOCUMENTATION REFERENCES)
American laws prohibit the act of taking someone else's life.	Persons who commit mercy killings are subject to prosecution for murder or manslaughter. Many people go to jail for ending a loved one's suffering.	Dr. John Kraai injected a fatal dose of insulin into a patient and was charged with murder. Rosewell Gilbert fired two bullets into his terminally ill wife's head and was found guilty of murder and sentenced to life in prison.
Medical miracles happen frequently.	Doctors can perform heart transplants, which were impossible five years ago. People have revived from lengthy comas.	Baby Jan underwent a heart transplant and still survives. Baby Fay, who received a baboon heart, was kept alive for several days. Mike Paciola was in a coma for three years and was revived.
There would be potential for abuse of legalized euthanasia.	People would take advantage of mercy killing once it is accepted by society. It is not for us to judge the value of someone's life.	People might be able to get rid of unwanted, ill relatives. "The needle which would end a person's life may be put into the hands of people who have personal gain as their primary motive." Karen Quinlan remained in a coma with a respirator for 10 years.

EXAMPLE: DEFENSIVE DEBATE MATRIX

Team: Negative

Proposition: A Person Should Have the Right to Take His or Her Own Life if He or She is Terminally Ill.

MAIN IDEAS	SUPPORTING IDEAS	DETAILS/EXAMPLES (DOCUMENTATION REFERENCES)
New technology can save and prolong human life.	People can be kept alive until proper surgery can be performed or transplant organs can be found. Medical miracles happen.	Baby Fay was kept alive after receiving a baboon heart. Baby Jan received a heart from another baby and is alive. Heart transplants were impossible 5 years ago. Now many examples, even of heart/lung transplants.
Euthanasia is illegal.	American law prohibits mercy killing in all cases.	"Persons who commit euthanasia are subject to criminal prosecution for manslaughter or murder (e.g. *NY* v *Sharon, FLA.* v *Adams, NY* v *Kraii, FLA.* v *Gilbert*).
Removing a patient from a respirator violates the patient's rights.	U.S. law protects the rights of individuals. Lack of response does not confer permission or delegate decision. Medicine is to save rather than to destroy.	U.S. Statute A-3908 Bill of Rights "Most patients in this state are incompetent to make the decision to end their lives. Fear, pain, and guilt create feelings of overwhelming depression and guilt. Death is perceived as the only way out." Hippocratic Oath

EXAMPLE: ATTACK-STRATEGY MATRIX

Team: Negative

Proposition: A Person Should Have the Right to Take His or Her Own Life if He or She is Terminally Ill.

OPPONENTS' STRONG POINTS	ATTACK STRATEGY
A terminally ill person has the right to take his or her own life.	A terminally ill person should not have the right to take his or her life because the law prohibits euthanasia.
Machines keep lives going without regard to quality of life.	Machines prolong human lives until transplant organs or corrective surgery can be performed.
The general public is in favor of euthanasia.	Mercy killing is a criminal offense and people can be charged with murder or manslaughter.

OPPONENTS' WEAK POINTS	ATTACK STRATEGY
It is a human right to choose a quick death rather than a prolonged, painful one.	Suffering individuals may not be able to make a rational decision.
A close relative should have the right to decide to end the life of a family member who is terminally ill or comatose.	People may use mercy killing as a way to get rid of unwanted relatives or as a way to gain financially from their deaths.

NOW YOU DO IT

With your debate partner prepare three matrices for your proposition: Offensive, defensive, and attack strategy matrices.

Rules of Debate

With your partner, decide on your strategy as you review the roles and speaking order of each member of the debate team.

First Affirmative Speaker:

- ☐ Introduces the proposition
- ☐ Presents some of the stronger and the weakest arguments of the *affirmative* side
- ☐ Begins arguments against the *negative* side

First Negative Speaker:

- ☐ Introduces the *negative side* of the proposition
- ☐ Repairs any damage done by *first affirmative speaker*
- ☐ Presents *strong negative* arguments (no weak ones)
- ☐ Argues against the *affirmative side*

Second Affirmative Speaker:

- ☐ Repairs any damage done by the *negative* side
- ☐ Foresees and covers any arguments that the *negative* side may use against the *affirmative* side
- ☐ Argues against the *negative* side

☐ Presents *strongest affirmative* arguments
☐ Summarizes and concludes the *affirmative* presentation

Second Negative Speaker:

☐ Repairs any damage done by the *affirmative* side
☐ Argues against the *affirmative* side
☐ Presents remaining *negative* arguments
☐ Summarizes and concludes the *negative* presentation

| 1st Affirmative | → | 1st Negative | → | 2nd Affirmative | → | 2nd Negative |

Notice that each speaker has a particular role in the debate and must present specific information. The *first affirmative* is the first person to speak and does not have to respond to what others say. Therefore, only this speaker may have a prepared speech. Having a prepared speech, however, does not mean reading it from a paper. Other speakers must not only know their information thoroughly but must be able to listen to their opponents and answer their arguments while presenting necessary information.

This is why strategy becomes so important. You must meet with your partner to decide which are your strong and weak arguments and who will present which information.

As you did your library research, you wrote all your information on index cards. Now you will see why. As you determine with your partner in which order to present your information, simply arrange the index cards in that order. When you are finished, your index cards will be in the order you intend to use them when you debate. This way, you will not have to do any rewriting.

Selecting Visual Aids

Visual aids can add interest and power to your presentation. Some commonly used types of visual aids are:

☐ Slides
☐ Charts
☐ Graphs
☐ Transparencies
☐ Posters
☐ Photographs
☐ Three-dimensional objects

However, keep these things in mind when using visual aids:

□ Make sure they are large enough to be seen by everyone in the room.
□ Limit information on charts, posters, or transparencies to one or two ideas.
□ Make your materials look professional.
□ Use bright colors.
□ Do not pass objects during your presentation.
□ Do not "read" from visuals or turn your back to the audience.
□ Practice with your visuals before your presentation.
□ Do not reveal your visuals until you are ready to use them.
□ Try out your equipment (projectors, etc.) before your presentation.
□ Remove transparencies from the projector (and turn if off) when you are finished.

With your partner, plan when and where to use visual aids. Carefully select what you will present and how you will use it. Make sure you practice with these visual aids with your partner before your debate. "Practice" means actually going through the debate as you use the visuals. This will give you confidence and help you pace your presentation.

TIPS ON MAKING AN EFFECTIVE PRESENTATION

1. Look at the people in the audience when you are speaking rather than over their heads or at your notes. Eye contact is important.
2. Use visual aids to create interest and to underline your arguments.
3. Be very familiar with your information so you can respond quickly and accurately.
4. Dress to make a good impression on your audience.
5. Do not use filler words such as "well," "uh . . . ," "you know."
6. Speak in a calm, confident voice at a normal rate of speed. When people are nervous, they often speak rapidly or mumble.
7. Practice your presentation aloud with your partner. This will help you sequence your presentation and gain confidence.

The Debate

With your partner, decide who will go first and who will go second. Each of you will have a minimum of 3 minutes and a maximum of 4 minutes to debate. You each have only one opportunity to speak. Be sure that you know your material well. Rehearse it until you are comfortable with it. Remember that in a debate, you do not read a prepared statement unless you are the *first affirmative speaker*, and even then, you should speak to your audience rather than read. You speak and respond to your opponents. If you have a great deal of material, 4 minutes will seem like a very short amount of time. However, if you don't have much information, 3 minutes will seem very long.

Arrive early to class on the day of the debate so you can do the following:

☐ Put your proposition on the blackboard.
☐ List the names of the *affirmative* and the *negative teams*.
☐ Arrange four chairs at the front of the classroom.
☐ Set up your visual aids (but don't show them).
☐ Check and adjust the focus of your audiovisual equipment.
☐ Arrange your notes on your desk so you can easily access information.

Before the debate, the class will vote on the proposition. This way the debaters will know how many people support, oppose, or are neutral to the proposition. Remember, these people are your audience. Your job is to convince them to support your side of the proposition.

The instructor will appoint a timekeeper to let the speakers know how much time has elapsed during their speech. The timekeeper should sit in a place which can be seen easily by the debaters. After the presenter has spoken 2 minutes, the timekeeper should put up two fingers. After 3 minutes, he should put up three fingers. After 4 minutes, he should wave his hand once to indicate that no more time remains for the speaker. At this point, the speaker may complete a sentence but must stop even if he or she has not provided all the information.

When the debate is finished, the instructor will ask the class to vote again: once to determine if they have changed in their support of the proposition and once to decide which team did the best job during the debate. If time remains, your instructor will allow the audience to ask questions and to comment on the debate.

Writing the Research Paper

By now, you know your information very well. Not only have you done research on the subject, but you have also had an opportunity to test your ideas and information through debate. From the debate you may see a need to do more research or to rework or reorganize some of the information before writing the research paper. Because you are so familiar with your subject, it will be easy for you to put it into a research paper. Use the same organizational technique you used for the debate. Sort your index cards in the order in which you want to present the information. (This may not be the same order that you used in the debate.) Use an *organizational matrix* to guide your writing.

Sample Research Paper

On the following pages is a sample research paper and bibliography. Take time to read it carefully to see how the writer uses quotes and creates a logical argument supported by specific, concrete details.

Please note that this paper is not a perfect research paper. It is presented here as a teaching tool which may be used in a variety of ways.

1. Your teacher may grade it as if a student in the class had submitted it. Then, he or she may use the research paper to discuss the errors and indicate the paper's strengths and weaknesses to you. In this way you will know what your instructor considers when grading a paper and what elements are important in assigning a grade.
2. Your instructor may assign parts of the paper to the class to read, comment on and correct. (This may be done in connection with work studied in the "Error Correction\Reference Section.")
3. Your instructor may ask you to evaluate and grade the entire research paper. Some items to consider as you go through the research paper are listed below:
   a. Does it have a well-defined thesis?
   b. Is there sufficient documentation to support or prove the thesis?
   c. Are the arguments well-developed and logical?
   d. Are the citations properly written?
   e. Is the language clear and grammatically correct?
   f. Are there errors in spelling or punctuation?
   g. Is there an appropriate introduction and conclusion?
   h. Is the bibliography properly presented?
   i. Other questions that your instructor may wish to include.

   _____

   _____

   _____

   _____

   _____

   _____

   _____ _____

   _____

When you have finished, your instructor will discuss the research paper with your class and will review the directions for developing and writing your research paper.

HANDGUN CONTROL:
A NECESSITY FOR SURVIVAL

Name: _____

Course: _____
Instructor's name: _____
Date: _____

For the past twenty years gun control has become a touchy issue in the United States. Within the past decade handgun control in particular has become a hot issue of debate on Capitol Hill. The concern this shows is well warranted too. Nearly every day headlines are filled with a tale of murder. More often than not these murders are committed with handguns. And with every such murder the question is asked what can be done. The answer is simple. The use and possession of handguns by the general public should be made illegal. Of course, this statement is made with the understanding that this does not apply to the military or the police forces. The underlying issues in the debate for handgun control include: Second Amendment Rights, the right to defense, the use of handguns in hunting and recreation, and most important, the use of handguns in crime and violence.

The National Rifle Association has stated, "Laws prohibiting the ownership of guns, restricting their use, or requiring the gun owner to license or register a gun are regarded by gun owners as unnecessary restrictions and threats to their Constitutional Rights" (Leddy 2). According to the Bureau of Justice Statistics gun owners did not think that gun laws were "unnecessary restrictions. . . ." In fact, of those people stating that they did own a gun 31% said they would favor banning the sale and possession of handguns in their community. Further, 26% of all handgun owners surveyed said they would favor the same thing (111).

NRA's claim that gun control legislation is considered by most to be a threat to their Constitutional Rights may also be untrue. Results of DMI (Decision Making Information) and Caddell Surveys of 1978 both agree that most Americans do not feel that gun control is a violation of their Constitutional (Second Amendment) Rights (qtd. in Wright 226–31).

The Second Amendment states, "A well regulated militia being necessary to the security of a free state, the right of the people shall not be infringed." To understand the exact meaning of this Amendment it must be viewed within the context in which it was written. When this was written our nation had no formal army so citizens were expected to fight in the militia. For this to be possible each citizen needed to be armed (Bennett 285). Furthermore, Martin Ashman, Attorney, clarified the intent of the Second Amendment by saying, "The circumstances surrounding the adoption and ratification of the U.S. Constitution and its Second Amendment . . . reflect debate over the proper balance of power between State and Federal Government with respect to armed forces—and not over a right to arms for any individual purpose" (Ashman 97–111).

The United States Supreme Court, however, has yet to rule on the precise meaning of the "militia clause." Although in United States vs. Cruikshank (1876) the court upheld, "private

ownership of arms . . . was not a right guaranteed by the
Constitution." And, the Seventh Circuit Court of Appeals in
Chicago ruled, "The possession of handguns by individuals *is not* a
part of the right to keep and bear arms" ("Guns in America"
938).

Many people feel, though, that they have the right to defend
themselves, and that prohibiting the use and possession of
handguns will in many ways reduce their potential in this
respect. Of those people surveyed by the Bureau of Justice, 20%
stated that the reason they owned a firearm was for defense
(109). This study also showed that 68% of those people owning a
firearm said they would try to use it in defense against a burglar.
Based on these claims maybe the use of handguns in self defense
is a valid argument for anti-control. In reality these claims are
not worth the paper they're written on. A Caddell Survey
(Cambridge Reports Inc., Patrick Caddell Political Polling Firm)
found that only 26% of handgun owners have ever carried the
gun outside the home for protection or self-defense. Of this
percentage only 3% have ever used it for protection (qtd. in
Wright 143).

A study by Dr. Arthur Kellerman relates the specific results of
owning a gun. Kellerman, then a student at the University of
Washington School of Medicine, found that of 398 killings in gun-
owning households, 84% were suicides, 10% were homicides
during family arguments, 3% were accidents, while only 2% were
self-protection, and a mere 0.5% were actual burglars ("Guns").
This means that for each incidence of self-defense homicide, 1.3
accidental gunshot deaths, and 4.6 criminal homicides (most of
which were relatives or aquaintances), resulted ("Homeguard").
With these things in mind it is logical to assume that a handgun
at home, whether it is used for protection or not, will more likely
result in the death or injury of a family member than a burglar or
other potential offender.

In the same vein, 65% of all gun owners state that the reason
for owning a firearm is for recreation (109); where recreational
purposes include, hunting and target shooting. These so called
recreational guns result in approximately 800 accidental deaths
each year not including the number of people maimed or
seriously injured ("Guns in America" 933). Thus, it is probable
that a recreation gun will result in death or harm to somebody.

These statistics on self-defense and recreational handguns
alone should convince most people of their potential danger *and*
that they should be eliminated in the United States; however, if
they don't, consider the widespread use of handguns in crime and
violence.

Some gun control advocates contend that guns are a cause of
crime. Psychological studies have shown that "Firearms,
especially handguns, give potential offenders the courage (and

means) to do what they would otherwise not be capable of doing"
(Wright). Most people agree this conclusion is valid. Whether this
is true or not, though, is of no consequence—whether they cause
crime or not, it is true that gun crimes require guns, and guns,
predominantly handguns, are involved in the largest portion of
crime and violence in the United States. Handguns, for instance,
are the leading instrument of murder in the U.S. FBI Uniform
Crime Reports for the years 1982–1986 show that 44% of all
murders were committed with a handgun. This is more than
double the amount of murders committed by the second leading
instrument of murder—cutting and stabbing instruments,
accounting for 21% of all murders in the U.S. (UCR10).

Handguns account for 73% of all murders committed with
firearms in general, such as rifles and shotguns. Evidence
supports that the concealability is the discriminating element
between crime and noncrime guns. Approximately 75% of all
crime guns have barrel lengths of three inches or less; i.e.,
handguns (Wright 17). One can only imagine the pronounced
decrease in murder alone if handguns were eliminated.

Nonetheless, anti-control advocates contend that even if
handguns are made illegal for the law-abiding citizen, criminals
will still be able to obtain them. This is true. Still, one must stop
to consider where criminals are obtaining guns under the
existing conditions of limited handgun control. Many weapons
used in crime are weapons stolen from law-abiding citizens
(Wright 140). By making it illegal for the general public to use
and possess handguns one source of criminally obtained weapons
would be eliminated. Moreover, accidental deaths and injuries due
to handguns would be virtually removed.

Under the Gun Control Act of 1968 an approximate increase of
65 million firearms has been observed. This is roughly double the
amount of firearms in this country prior to ratification of this
law. At the same time incidence of crime and violence involving
guns has also increased. Evidently, existing federal gun control
legislation is ineffective. Even the federal government admits to
the general ineptitude of the Gun Control Act of 1968. According
to Public Law PL-308, enacted on May 19 1986, "Additional
legislation is required to reaffirm the intent of the Congress, in
section 101 of the Gun Control Act of 1968" (U.S. Code 449).

There is some evidence that through gun control legislation
gun-related crimes can be reduced (Wright 308). In places where
handgun-control legislation have been introduced a decrease in
crime and violence have been observed. The Bartley-Fox
Amendment of 1974 did essentially two things. It expanded
Massachusetts licensing procedures and made unlicensed
carrying of firearms an offense punishable with a mandatory
sentence of one year. A study by Pierce and Bowers (1979) found
that under this amendment gun assaults decreased. Additionally,

armed robberies and gun homicides were moderately decreased (qtd. in Wright 291).

In hopes of seeing the same results many other communities nationwide have initiated similar legislation. For instance, Morton Grove, Oak Park, and Evanston, three Chicago suburbs, have banned new handguns from their jurisdiction. Washington, DC, has done the same. And in 1982 a San Francisco law requires owners to give up their handguns ("Guns in America" 938). Apparently the need and desire for handgun control is seen as necessary to many, many people in the United States.

Currently it is estimated that there are 120 million firearms in private hands ("Homeguard" 68). This figure indicates that the weapons arsenal among the general public in the United States is certainly greater than that of any other nation. Violence, violent crime specifically, is also much more frequent in the United States (Wright 1–2). More importantly, the number of guns in this nation is increasing. "The prospect of citizens preparing to shoot one another is something that any civilized nation would try to avoid . . . something must be done to stem the flow of weapons into private hands" (Wright 82). That "something" is prohibiting the use and possession of handguns to the general public.

BIBLIOGRAPHY

Ashman, Martin C. "Handgun Control by Local Government," *Northern Kentucky Law Review,* No. 1, 1982, pp 97–111.

"Guns in America: The Debate Continues." *Editorial Research Reports* Washington, D.C., 1985.

"Guns at Home—Do They Protect." *US News and World Report.* 23 June 1986: 100:9.

"Homeguard (Deaths From Household Firearms)." *Scientific American* Sept. 1986: 255: 68.

Leddy, Edward F. *Magnum Force Lobby, The National Rifle Association Fights Gun Control.* New York: University Press of America, Inc. 1987.

Sourcebook of Criminal Justice Statistics: Bureau of Justice Statistics. Washington: U.S. Department of Justice Statistics, 1986.

Uniform Crime Reports for the United States. Washington: U.S. Department of Justice, 1986.

United States. U.S. Code Congressional and Administrative News. *Interstate Transportation of Firearms.* 99th Cong., 2nd sess. Washington: GPO, 1986.

Wright, James D., et al. *Under the Gun: Weapons Crime, and Violence in America.* New York: Aldine Publishing Co., 1983.

Eleven

Error Correction/ Reference Section

Editing and error correction are crucial parts of writing. In this section, we will examine:

☐ Ways to cut your writing time
☐ Use of the thesaurus and dictionary
☐ Spelling rules
☐ Review of word and verb forms
☐ Review of verb tense
☐ Recognition and correction of common errors in grammar, punctuation, and sentence structure
☐ Recognition and correction of wording errors
☐ Editing techniques
☐ Proofreading techniques

This section is intended as a guide to help you identify and correct errors. For additional exercises, your instructor will refer you to other textbooks and workbooks or will work with you individually.

Five Ways to Cut Your Writing Time

One of the most important aspects of writing is planning. This can save you an amazing amount of time and irritation. As we have discussed in the main text of this book, there are five common sense steps in this process:

1. Spend time *thinking* before you write. Use the act of writing your first draft to help you think.

As silly as this may seem, many people just begin writing without taking time to analyze the topic and think their first draft is the final essay! Analyze the topic to decide what the writer must provide to answer the question.

2. Decide on your purpose *first*.

The next step is to decide on your purpose: what you want the reader to do, to know, or to expect. By identifying exactly what you intend to cover and accomplish, you will give direction to your essay and make the development process simpler.

3. Plan your presentation strategy.

Decide next on the most effective way to present your information. This requires you to analyze both your topic and your audience. Which format will work best for your topic: comparison and contrast, persuasive, or the informative format? How can you begin your essay in a way that will interest your reader? How much knowledge does your reader have about the topic? How much and what kind of information should you include to meet your reader's needs?

4. Use a matrix or other organizational device to align your main points and supporting material.

Using a matrix will ensure that you gather the required information to support your topic. This will also help you organize your material from the reader's point of view.

5. Edit ruthlessly *after* you finish your first draft.

Many students break their train of thought by editing each sentence as they write. Wait until you have finished the first draft to edit your work.

Using a Dictionary

One of the best tools a writer can use is the dictionary. A dictionary can tell you many things. Look at the entry below:

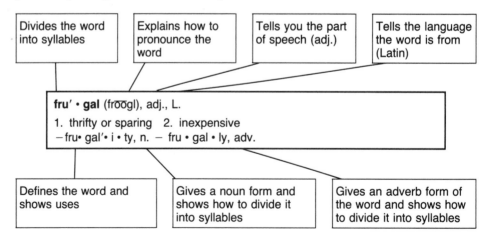

As you can see, the dictionary tells many things about a word: its part of speech, correct use, spelling, and syllables.

John must be *frugal* because he saves coupons to use when buying groceries.

His *frugality* is recognized by his co-workers because he never goes out to eat.

He *frugally* takes a sandwich to work with him everyday instead of going to the office cafeteria.

Everyone knows of John's *frugality*.

As a further guide, here are some commonly used abbreviations for the parts of speech:

n.   noun   *Example:* dog, moss, receiver

v.   verb

vt.   verb transitive. This means that the verb requires an object.
Example: The thief (noun) *stole* (verb) the television set (object).

vi.   verb intransitive. This means the verb cannot take an object
Example: The two children *misbehaved* during church.

adj.   adjective   *Example:* worldly, beautiful, cohesive

adv.   adverb   *Example:* quickly, cohesively, rapidly

pron.   pronoun   *Example:* you, everyone, it, somebody

conj.   conjunction   *Example:* but, and, or, nor

prep.   preposition   *Example:* of, before, from

interj.   interjection   *Example:* oh, well

Spelling

Spelling in English can be very difficult. Many times words are not spelled as they are pronounced. For example, the word "through" is pronounced "thru." One word may also sound like another word with a very different meaning. For example, "read" sounds like "reed." Although the spelling rules below will help you decide how to spell a word, always take the time to look up in the dictionary words you are uncertain how to spell.

SPELLING RULES

1. When spelling words that have both an "e" and an "i" together, remember

"i" before "e" except after "c" or when pronounced a as in n*ei*ghbor and w*ei*gh.

Examples: bel**ie**ve
rec**ei**ve

2. Words with an "e" at the end change the sound of the preceding vowel. Notice the different pronunciation for t*a*pe and t*a*p. The "e" at the end makes the vowel "say" its name.

When you change these words by adding "ed" or "ing," remember this rule. To keep the sound of the vowel, double the last letter if the word does not end in "e." If the word ends in "e," remove the "e" and add the ending.

Examples: tap/tapping   tape/taping
hop/hopping   hope/hoping
star/starring   stare/staring

3. When you come to the end of a line and you need to divide a word, always divide the word by syllables. If you do not know where the syllables end, look in your dictionary. You will see a • between groups of letters. This dot is used to identify syllables.

Look up the following words in your dictionary and divide them by syllables by placing a space between each syllable.

independently
recreation
absolutely
unconditionally
radioactive
childhood
fight
watched

Using the Thesaurus

An excellent place to find descriptive words is the *thesaurus*. A thesaurus is different from a dictionary. A thesaurus gives synonyms so the writer can choose the most specific, effective word. In the dictionary section, you learned the different forms for the word "frugal," how to divide them into syllables, and what part of speech each is.

In the thesaurus, you would see the following entry for "frugal":

frugal, adj. prudent, saving, provident, thrifty; sparing, stinting. See ECONOMY, MODERATION. Ant., see WASTE

In the above entry, "adj." means adjective. The words which follow are words which are close in meaning to "frugal." They do not mean exactly the same thing *nor can they be used interchangeably.* "Ant." means antonym, words which have an opposite meaning.

The capitalized words have similar or opposite meanings; under their entries, additional words that may apply to "frugal" are listed.

Use the thesaurus when you are looking for a word that means the same thing as another word. The thesaurus can also help you find another word to replace a word you have already used once or to find a more precise word.

There is one very important thing you should know about words in the thesaurus. If you are not completely sure of the meaning, *look it up before you use it!* Otherwise you may end up with an unintentionally humorous sentence.

Use the thesaurus to find other words for the following:

1. nice
2. nervous
3. forest
4. forgive
5. attack
6. erase
7. seldom

Word Forms

DEFINING WORD FORMS

Errors in word forms usually occur because students focus on the meaning of the word and don't pay attention to the word's form or part of speech. By "part of speech," we mean whether the word is a noun, verb, adjective, adverb, etc. This information, which you can find in the dictionary, tells you how to use the word. Consider this example:

I can *collect* many things.

My *collection* may be extensive.

Collectors collect many types of *collectibles*.

If you were to look up these words in your dictionary, you would see the following:

collect v., to gather things of a similar type

collectibles n., the things people collect or gather

collection n., the name given to a group of things a person collects

collector n., the name given to a person who collects things

Notice that three of these words have "n." next to them, indicating that they are nouns. However, each is used differently because, although it refers to collecting, each has a different meaning.

Because of the diversity of word forms in English, it is easy to make mistakes like those in the sentences listed below. Identify the error in each and correct it.

I can adjust myself to the cultural here.

I would like to be an electrical engineering.

USING CORRECT WORD FORMS

As we have seen, one word in English may assume several forms. Look at the words listed below. Do you know how to use each in a sentence? If you don't, check your dictionary. Then write a sentence for each word.

1. administer _____

_____

administration _____

_____

adminstrator _____

_____

administrative _____

_____

2. reflect _____

_____

reflection _____

_____

reflective _____

_____

reflector _____

_____

3. defend _____

_____

defendant _____

_____

defended _____

_____

defender _____

_____

defenseless _____

_____

defensively _____

_____

Verb Forms

In English, verbs have several forms and may be regular or irregular. Some verbs take the present, past, and participle form. The following table will discuss these verb forms:

PRESENT	PAST	PARTICIPLE
Add 's' to all forms of the verbs below if the subject is he, she, or it or a word that can be substituted for he, she, or it. He *flies* airplanes. This plane *flies* well. (it)	For most verbs, add "ed." Words in the verb table are irregular. He *finished* the essay.	This form is always used with a helping verb, e.g., *has* beaten, *will have* done, *might have* slept, *had* sunk. Sometimes when people say contractions, it's hard to hear the helping verb, e.g., She*'s* gone, I*'ve* spoken
VERB	VERB + ED	HELPING VERB + VERB + ED or EN
OR _____ VERB + S	OR AS SHOWN IN TABLE ON PAGE 192.	ING Verbs used to show a continuing action. Use the helping verb + the verb + 'ing' I *am reading* a book. We *are leaving* after class. I *was reading* a book.
		AM + VERB + ING IS + VERB + ING ARE + VERB + ING WAS + VERB + ING WERE + VERB + ING

IRREGULAR VERBS

Present	Past	Past Participle* (use with has, have, or had and with passives)	Present	Past	Past Participle* (use with has, have, or had and with passives)
am, are, is	was, were	been	hear	heard	heard
beat	beat	beat(en)	hide	hid	hidden
become	became	become	hit	hit	hit
begin	began	begun	hold	held	held
bend	bent	bent	hurt	hurt	hurt
bet	bet	bet	keep	kept	kept
bite	bit	bitten	know	knew	known
bleed	bled	bled	lay	laid	laid
blow	blew	blown	lead	led	led
break	broke	broken	leave	left	left
breed	bred	bred	lend	lent	lent
bring	brought	brought	let	let	let
build	built	built	lose	lost	lost
buy	bought	bought	lie	lay	lain
catch	caught	caught	make	made	made
choose	chose	chosen	mean	meant	meant
come	came	come	meet	met	met
cost	cost	cost	pay	paid	paid
creep	crept	crept	put	put	put
cut	cut	cut	quit	quit	quit
do	did	done	read	read	read
dig	dug	dug	ride	rode	ridden
draw	drew	drawn	ring	rang	rung
drink	drank	drunk	rise	rose	risen
drive	drove	driven	say	said	said
eat	ate	eaten	see	saw	seen
fall	fell	fallen	seek	sought	sought
feed	fed	fed	sell	sold	sold
feel	felt	felt	send	sent	sent
fight	fought	fought	set	set	set
find	found	found	shake	shook	shaken
flee	fled	fled	shoot	shot	shot
fly	flew	flown	shut	shut	shut
forget	forgot	forgot(ten)	sing	sang	sung
forgive	forgave	forgiven	sink	sank	sunk
freeze	froze	frozen	sit	sat	sat
get	got	got(ten)	sleep	slept	slept
give	gave	given	slide	slid	slid
go	went	gone	speak	spoke	spoken
grind	ground	ground	spend	spent	spent
grow	grew	grown	spin	spun	spun
hang	hung	hung	split	split	split
have	had	had	spread	spread	spread

Present	Past	Past Participle* (use with has, have, or had and with passives)	Present	Past	Past Participle* (use with has, have, or had and with passives)
			tear	tore	torn
spring	sprang	sprung	tell	told	told
stand	stood	stood	think	thought	thought
steal	stole	stolen	throw	threw	thrown
stick	stuck	stuck	understand	understood	understood
strike	struck	struck	wake up	woke up	woken up
swear	swore	sworn	wear	wore	worn
sweep	swept	swept	weave	wove	woven
swim	swam	swum	weep	wept	wept
swing	swung	swung	win	won	won
take	took	taken	wind	wound	wound
teach	taught	taught	wring	wrung	wrung

*The past participle is never used alone. It must be used with a helping verb. For example,
He *has slept* for three hours.
They *were gone* until dawn.
His testimony *was sworn* in court.
The politician *had* already *chosen* his campaign advisors.

Verb Tense

Verb tense is difficult to understand because it is complex. To help you understand how the different verb tenses are used and formed, please read the chart below. It is the history of an essay in progress.

1. After I *had written* the thesis sentence, my ideas flowed.

    PAST PERFECT

    One past activity is completed before the other begins.

    Had + verb + 3rd form

2. Of course, I *had been trying* to write a thesis sentence for 2 hours.

    PAST PERFECT CONTINUOUS

    A complete past action that was done over a period of time.

    Had + been + verb + ing

---

3. In fact, while I *was writing*, two friends asked me to go to the movies with them.

    PAST CONTINUOUS

    A past activity which the person was in the process of doing when another past activity happened.

    Was + verb + ing
    or
    Were

4. Of course, I said no.

    SIMPLE PAST

    Action done in the past.

    verb + ed or irregular form

---

5. I *have completed* my opening paragraph.

    PRESENT PERFECT

    An action started in the past and completed in the present.

    Have + verb + 3rd form
    or
    Has

6. I *have been working* on the body paragraphs for the past hour.

    PRESENT PERFECT CONTINUOUS

    An action started in the past and continuing into the present.

    Have + been + verb + ing

---

7. Finally, I *am working* on the conclusion.

    PRESENT CONTINUOUS

    An action continuing in the present.

    Am + verb + ing
    or
    Is
    or
    Are

8. I *will have been working* on my essay for 3 hours.

    FUTURE PERFECT

    An action begun in the past to be completed in the future.

    Will + have + been + verb + ing

---

9. My writing *is* better because I *write* in my journal daily.

    PRESENT

    An action done in the present.

    Verb
    or
    Verb + s

10. Tomorrow I *will hand* in my essay.

    FUTURE

    An action to be done in the future.

    Will + verb

---

11. I hope that at the end of the week I *will be celebrating* an "A."

    FUTURE CONTINUOUS

    An action to continue in the future.

    Will + be + verb + ing

12. If that happens, I *will have achieved* my fondest dream—an "A" in English composition!

    FUTURE PERFECT

    An action to be done and completed in the future.

    Will + have + verb + 3rd form

Infinitives

The *infinitive* is the word "to" plus the verb. Some examples are:

to stand

to expect

to run

to say

The infinitive is used when two main verbs come together. For example:

I want *to pass* the exam.

He wants *to work* overtime.

She said *to come* early.

The infinitive in each sentence above answers the verb's question:

Want what?   To pass

Want what?   To work

Said what?   To come

INFINITIVE EXERCISE

Complete the following sentences.

1. He passed _____ he could do it. (prove)
2. Janet worked _____ her college tuition. (pay)
3. The state government reduced the speed limit _____ fuel. (save)

Answer the following questions with complete sentences. Be sure to use an infinitive in your sentences.

1. What did she tell him?
2. What did Martha tell George?
3. What did he want to accomplish?
4. Why did the Department of Transportation expand the bridge?

Word Order

DEFINING WORD ORDER

Some languages have no requirements for a definite word order. Words may be used in any order without changing the meaning or causing confusion. This is not so in English. Look at the two sentences below and determine what each of the sentences mean and why the meaning changes.

I had milk chocolate.

I had chocolate milk.

In sentence one "chocolate" is a noun and "milk" is describing the type of chocolate it is. In sentence two "milk" is the noun and "chocolate" is describing the milk.

There is a definite order for presenting words in English. Most sentences begin with the subject and are followed by a verb and then the object. The subject tells who or what did, is doing, or will do the action, and the object completes the thought.

Subject + **verb** + **object**

The fifteen-year-old | was drawing | an elaborate picture.

Notice that the subject and object parts of the sentence may have more than one part of speech—e.g., nouns and adjectives.

Often students have difficulty knowing in what order to put these nouns and adjectives. The chart below will outline the word order to use with nouns and adjectives.

DETERMINER	OPINION	PHYSICAL DESCRIPTION				NATIONALITY	NOUN
		SIZE	SHAPE	AGE	COLOR		
A	powerful		muscular		white	Arabian	stallion
An	elegant		round		diamond		ring
Two				old		Italian	men
Her	pretty	little					umbrella
A	clear				blue		sky

USING CORRECT WORD ORDER

Using the table, rearrange the words in the following sentences.

1. childish a young man demanded attention waiter from the.

_____

2. small Irish in the town villager the waited for old the fisherman.

_____

3. pieces two sweet chocolate of rolled on dirty floor the old.

_____

4. valve the turn until hear you click the.

_____

5. barked viciously passerby dog the black curly little at the.

_____

Articles

USING ARTICLES

Many languages do not have articles, like "a," "the," and "an." As a result, these articles often confuse nonnative speakers. Articles are used in English to tell the reader if the item being discussed is a particular item or just any item.

Rules for Article Use

1. **A:**

> I want *a* good book to read.

This means that the person will read *any* good book.

> I want *the* good book you told me about.

This means that the person wants a *particular* book, the one the writer was told about.

2. **A and An:**

A and *an* are used *only* with *singular* forms.

> I want *a* good book (correct—*one* book)
> I want *a* good books (incorrect—books is *plural*)

An is used with nouns, abbreviations, or modifiers which begin with vowels.

An error	A mistake
An apple	A pear
An integer	A number
An increasing debt	A large debt
An American flag	A flag
An IBM product	A Kodak product

3. **The:**

The can be used with both singular and plural forms but refers to a specific item.

> I want *the* good books you told me about. (specific books)

4. **No article:**

Sometimes no article is needed. Consider these sentences:

- ☐ Books are fun to read.
- ☐ Children can be both annoying and entertaining.
- ☐ Nature is spectacular this time of year.

Notice that no article is needed because each of these sentences is a *generalization*. Plural nouns and/or non-count nouns are usually found in generalizations. To generalize is to speak in broad terms about something. When a noun refers to all items in a category, do not use an article.

5. **Non-count nouns:**

Some words that can be counted in other languages cannot be counted in English. These words have the same form in both singular and plural.

Some of these words are:

furniture	rice
homework	mail
work	supervision
information	fruit
equipment	worth
advice	machinery

The article "a" is never used in front of these words. Instead you must say "some homework," "a piece of machinery," "some advice."

The names of countries that have the word "union" or "united" in them require the word "the."

Great Britain	the United Kingdom
America	the United States
the United Arab Emirates	
the Netherlands	
the Union of Soviet Socialist Republics (the USSR)	

A group of lakes or mountain ranges also requires the word "the" as do the names of rivers:

The Great Lakes	Mt. Rushmore
The Rockies	The Genesee River
The Pyrenees	The Mississippi River
Lake Ontario	The Amazon
Pike's Peak	

ARTICLE USE EXERCISE

Circle the correct articles in the sentences below.

1. Where is (a, the) book you were reading last night?
2. (A, An, The) American Legion is (a, an) organization of men and women who served in (a, an, the) United States military.
3. That is not (a, an, the) dress that I ordered.
4. Please answer (a, an, the) telephone.
5. Most of (a, an, the) people who attended the concert arrived on time.
6. (A, An, The) accountant made (a, an) error on my income tax.
7. (A, An, The) home office of Idea Bank Associates is located in Honeoye, (a, an, the) small town in upstate New York.
8. Bring the following things with you: (a, an, the) pen, (a, an, the) notebook, and (a, an, the) book *The Grapes of Wrath*.
9. (A, An, The) American flag and (a, an, the) Canadian flag should be flown at (a, an, the) same height.
10. (A, An, The) man who won (a, an, the) grand prize decided to take (a, an, the) trip around the world.

Pronouns and Antecedents

RULES

☐ All pronouns ending in "one" or "body" are singular and require a singular verb or possessive:

Example:

Everyone must finish *his* or *her* work before we can break for lunch.

☐ Be careful when phrases between the subject and verb obscure the number.

Example:

Across the street *is* a *pharmacy and a clinic.* (incorrect)
One of the employees have left the building. (incorrect)

☐ Be careful when using compound subjects or objects using "I" and "me" or "he" and "him," etc.

Example:

The work was done by Jim and *I.* (incorrect)
The work was done by Jim and me. (not myself)

☐ When using who/whom decide on the correct pronoun by substituting he for who and him for whom.

Example:

(Who, Whom) made this mess?
He made this mess. So . . .
Who made this mess?

PRONOUN AND ANTECEDENT EXERCISE

Read each sentence carefully. Choose one word to complete each sentence.

1. A number of us (is, are) going to the hockey game.
2. The report was written by George, Karl, and (I, me, myself).
3. Everyone who takes these courses (are, is) sure to improve (his, their) writing.
4. Each of Mary's sisters (is, are) making a gift for (her, their) mother.
5. Two of the features of the plan (is, are) on-the-job training and custom-designed instruction.
6. Anyone traveling to Orlando is taking a chance unless (she, they) make(s) hotel reservations.
7. She is the woman (who, whom) made the presentation on computer software at the convention.

Fragments

DEFINING SENTENCE FRAGMENTS

A *sentence fragment* is an incomplete sentence used incorrectly as a sentence. As you know, a *complete sentence* contains a subject and a verb and makes sense by itself. However, a *sentence fragment*, although it may contain a subject and a verb, does not contain a complete thought. It is generally part of the sentence which occurs either before or after it in the paragraph.

Consider this example:

If he would work harder. He could accomplish a great deal.

The phrase in italics is a *sentence fragment*. It does not contain a complete thought by itself although it does contain a subject (he) and a verb (would work harder). However, if you combine the sentence fragment with the sentence that follows it, you have a complete thought.

If he would work harder, he could accomplish a great deal.

Briefly, the test of a sentence is the question, "Does the sentence make sense by itself?" If not, the sentence is a fragment and requires additional information.

CORRECTING SENTENCE FRAGMENTS

There are two ways to correct sentence fragments:

1. Add additional information to complete the sentence's meaning.

   Example:

   > If you have time (fragment)

   > If you have time, *please enter this data into the computer.* (complete sentence)

2. Combine the sentence fragment with another related sentence.

   Example:

   > If you have time. (fragment) *Please enter this data into the computer.* (complete sentence)

   > If you have time, please enter this data into the computer. (complete sentence)

Sometimes, you can improve a sentence by editing information when you combine the sentence fragment with the complete sentence.

Example:

> If you need additional space to answer questions. (fragment) You can find extra space on the reverse side of the page. (complete sentence)

1. If you need additional space to answer the questions, you can find extra space on the reverse side of the page. (combined sentence)
2. If you need additional space to answer questions, use the back of the page. (edited combined sentence)

Notice that sentence 2 has the same meaning but is worded more concisely than sentence 1.

SENTENCE FRAGMENT EXERCISE

Read each sentence pair carefully. If the sentence is a *fragment*, either add additional information to complete its meaning or combine it with the sentence before or after it. After combining the sentences, edit the combined sentence for conciseness.

1. When you get to Old Stone Road. You will see the Stone Tolan House, a restored eighteenth-century farmhouse.
2. The American Beauty rose is a deep red rose. Which is the national flower of the United States.
3. Included in the package. A coat, a shirt, and two necklaces which I ordered from a mail order catalogue.
4. Because there had been no rain for six weeks. Many crops died.
5. Hand in your term paper. After you proofread it carefully.
6. When you are seeking a job. You need to have an excellent resume.
7. So he would arrive on time. Jim left home 20 minutes early.
8. Review all the reports. Check them for errors in content and mechanics.
9. Although there are many fast-food restaurants. The largest chains are McDonald's and Burger King.
10. Consider your answers carefully. Make certain that you answer all questions completely.

Run-On Sentences

DEFINING RUN-ON SENTENCES

A run-on sentence *(comma splice)* occurs when two complete sentences are joined by insufficient punctuation, usually a comma.

Example:

> He should work harder, he could accomplish a great deal.
>
> The fund raiser was very successful it raised $45,000 for the Heart Fund.

In both cases, two sentences are run together into one (therefore, the *run-on sentence*).

CORRECTING RUN-ON SENTENCES

The run-on sentence can be corrected in three ways.

1. Break the run-on sentence into two sentences.

   Example:

   > The fund raiser was very successful. It raised $45,000 for the Heart Fund.

2. Make the run-on sentence a compound sentence. A compound sentence is made up of two independent clauses joined either by a coordinating conjunction (and, but, or, for, nor) or by a semicolon (;).

   Example:

   > The fund raiser was very successful; it raised $45,000 for the Heart Fund. (semicolon)

   > The fund raiser was very successful, *and* it raised $45,000 for the Heart Fund. (coordinating conjunction)

3. Make the run-on sentence a complex sentence. A complex sentence is made up of an independent clause and one or more dependent clauses.

   Example:

   > If he worked harder (dependent clause), he could accomplish a great deal (independent clause).

   > The fund raiser was very successful (independent clause) because it raised over $45,000 for the Heart Fund (dependent clause).

RUN-ON SENTENCE EXERCISE

Revise each of these run-on sentences in two different ways.

1. I cannot go on vacation this year I don't have any vacation days left.

   _____

   _____

   _____

   _____

2. She came to the party, he left.

   _____

   _____

   _____

   _____

3. The apples will be very expensive this year, the drought damaged fruit and killed many orchards.

   _____

   _____

   _____

   _____

4. She was not at her desk she missed an important call.

_____

_____

_____

_____

5. Computers have revolutionized industry information can be transmitted to remote facilities through modems.

_____

_____

_____

_____

Choppy Sentences

DEFINING CHOPPY SENTENCES

Choppy sentences (stringiness) occur when the paragraph is made up of a series of very short, simple sentences. Although technically correct, these sentences make the writing seem "choppy" and abrupt. Consider this paragraph:

> Rochester, N.Y., is an industrial city. It is located in upstate New York. It is the corporate home of Eastman Kodak. Rochester is also the headquarters of Xerox.

As you can see, this paragraph contains four short sentences. However, it does not flow well.

CORRECTING CHOPPY SENTENCES

Choppy sentences can be corrected through *sentence combining*. To combine sentences, read each carefully and analyze its contents. Look for a relationship between the ideas in two or more of the sentences. Then combine the ideas by removing unnecessary information. Make sure the resulting sentence is complete and correct.

If you look at the paragraph above, you will see that sentences 1 and 2 are related and can be combined. Sentences 3 and 4 can also be combined. Here is a revised version:

> Rochester is an industrial city located in upstate New York. It is the corporate headquarters of Eastman Kodak and Xerox.

SENTENCE COMBINING EXERCISE

Combine each of these sentence pairs to create a complex or compound sentence.

1. The student bought his first car. It was a blue Chevrolet.

   _____

   _____

2. Our first child was born in October. Her name is Aimee Francesca.

   _____

   _____

4. The electrician retired in June. He had worked for the company for 35 years.

   _____

   _____

5. The chicken is put in a pressure cooker. It is cooked for 20 minutes.

   _____

   _____

6. The stereo was too loud. It disturbed the neighbors.

   _____

   _____

7. Construction areas are dangerous. You must wear a hard hat.

   _____

   _____

8. He did not graduate from high school. He had a difficult time getting a job.

   _____

   _____

9. The telephone rang. I was in the bathtub.

   _____

   _____

10. The Christmas party is on December 12. Everyone is invited.

   _____

   _____

Wordy Sentences (Wordiness)

DEFINING WORDINESS

Wordiness occurs when the writer either uses too many words to describe an idea or writes sentences which are too long and complex. Consider this example of wordiness:

It is important to be very careful to make sure that you plan your work before you begin so that you can make the most efficient use of your time.

If you analyze this sentence, you will see that many words and phrases are unnecessary or repetitive. For example, the first twelve words are unnecessary because they do not add important information to the main idea of the sentence. The phrase "before you begin" can be eliminated because *all* planning should be done before you begin. Therefore, this sentence can be written simply as:

Plan your work to use your time efficiently.

CORRECTING WORDINESS

To correct wordiness, you must eliminate unnecessary material from your sentences and be certain you do not include too many ideas within your sentence. Here are some common errors which cause wordiness:

☐ **Overuse of "it is" and "there are."** *There is* and *it is* are seldom necessary to the structure of the sentence and can be eliminated.

Example:

It is necessary to turn off the electricity before you work on the circuit-breaker box.

Correction:

Turn off the electricity before you work on the circuit-breaker box.

☐ **Linking too many phrases in a sentence.** This can be corrected by breaking the sentence into smaller, more concise sentences.

Example:

Rochester, N.Y., which is a large city in New York, is located on Lake Ontario, is the corporate home of Eastman Kodak and Xerox, has four major colleges, is known for its gardening, and has three waterfalls downtown.

Correction:

Rochester, a large city on Lake Ontario, is the corporate home of Eastman Kodak, Xerox, and four major colleges. This scenic city is known for its gardens and downtown waterfalls.

WORDINESS EXERCISE

Read the following paragraph carefully. Correct sentence structure errors and eliminate wordy sentences.

205

The success of any project depends on the attitude of company employees. They can determine whether a project succeeds or fails. Employees who are challenged by their work and have the opportunity for promotion tend to be more productive and creative than those who are bored or locked into a job. Not only do their attitudes reflect upon their productivity, it is likely that their bad attitudes will also spread discontent to other employees.

Passive Voice

DEFINITION OF PASSIVE VOICE

Many writers tend to overuse passive voice. This makes their writing less focused and, often, wordy. To determine what passive voice is, consider these two sentences:

> *Desks should be locked* when employees leave their office areas.
>
> *Employees should lock their desks* when they leave the office area.

The first sentence does not tell *who* should lock the desks. The person who will do the action is not named. This may create confusion. However, the second sentence contains a clear subject (employees) and verb (should lock). It is clear now who is responsible for the action.

Exceptions

There are three times when the writer may want to use passive voice:

1. When you are conveying unpopular information:

   A mistake was made when the sophomore was allowed to register for a graduate school class. (passive voice—blame is not directed toward a specific individual)

   The registrar made a mistake when he allowed the sophomore to register for a graduate school class. (active voice—the registrar is responsible for the action)

2. When the person is more important than the action:

   Ronald Reagan was elected president of the United States in 1980 and 1984. (passive voice—the president is the focus of this sentence, not the people who elected him)

   The American people elected Ronald Reagan by a landslide vote in 1980. (active voice—the American people took the action of electing Mr. Reagan)

3. When the doer of the action is unknown or unimportant.

   The new college campus was built in 1967.

   The Pyramids of Egypt were built thousands of years ago.

CORRECTING PASSIVE VOICE

To change a passive-voice sentence into an active-voice sentence, ask yourself, first, "What was done?" This will locate the verb or action word. Then, ask yourself, "Who did the action?" This will locate the subject of the sentence. The next step is to "turn the sentence around" so that the person who did the action becomes the *subject* of the sentence. Try this example:

Passive voice: The wedding dress was made by Mary's mother.

1. What was done? A wedding dress *was made.* (verb)
2. Who did it? Mary's mother.

Active voice: Mary's mother made the wedding dress.

PASSIVE-VOICE EXERCISE

1. The invoice was paid by Maxwell, Inc., on July 29.

2. This matter will be taken up by the Social Services Department.

3. Collateral was required by the bank to secure the loan.

4. An excellent dinner was prepared by Mr. John Martin, chef of the Honeoye Lake Inn.

5. The airline reservations were made by the travel agent.

6. A good time was had by all the people who attended the party.

7. The book was lost by a careless person.

8. Writing must be proofread thoroughly before it is handed in.

9. The orders for lunch will be taken by the office manager.

_____

_____

10. This work will be completed by the engineers by April 15.

_____

_____

Nonspecific Language

DEFINING NONSPECIFIC LANGUAGE

Often students use words that have multiple meanings or are not specific. This can confuse or mislead the reader. Consider this sentence:

Many students will have to pay considerably higher fees in the near future.

What questions do you have about this sentence? There are three unclear areas:

1. What students are affected?
2. How much is "considerably higher"?
3. When will the fee increase take place?

CORRECTING NONSPECIFIC LANGUAGE

The best way to correct nonspecific language which is caused by lack of information is to select words or information which present a clear picture to the reader. Let's correct the sentence above:

Students taking biochemistry laboratories (some students) will have to pay _an additional $125 in materials fees_ (more tuition) _when they register in September_ (the near future).

Sometimes, however, the student cannot think of the most effective word to describe an action or event.

Example:

Mr. Graves caught a _big_ fish in the St. John's River.

The word "big" is very nonspecific because it will be interpreted differently by each reader. For example, Mr. Graves may consider a "big" fish as one which weighs over 3 pounds. Another person may classify "big" as over 5 pounds. This is how misunderstandings over "fish stories" develop!

NONSPECIFIC LANGUAGE EXERCISE

Underline the nonspecific word or phrase. Then supply a concise, descriptive word to capture the meaning.

1. The salesperson said the car needed some work and was a little rusty.

   _____

   _____

2. I told the car dealer to paint the top of my truck white and the sides red.

   _____

   _____

3. She felt bad about what she had done.

   _____

   _____

4. He is a nice person to have around because he always has good ideas about things to do to have fun.

   _____

   _____

5. Stanley was described as a big, fat guy who treated people well.

   _____

   _____

6. That was a dumb thing to do because it caused a lot of problems.

   _____

   _____

7. I will meet you later down at the shopping center.

   _____

   _____

8. Go over to the warehouse and get me some wood to fix this platform.

   _____

   _____

9. "There isn't much on television this evening," she complained as she flipped through the *TV Guide*.

   _____

   _____

10. You can get into real trouble if you're not careful when you bid at an auction.

   _____

   _____

11. The owner said Spot was a good dog but that he had a rotten temper.

_____

_____

Redundant Wording

DEFINING REDUNDANT WORDING

Sometimes we overdo wording and use too many words to state an idea. The list below contains examples of redundant wording. The left column lists the incorrect phrases and the right column contains more concise forms.

Redundant Phrase	Concise Phrase
absolutely complete	complete
absolute truth	truth
actual experience	experience
adequate enough	enough
arrive on the scene	arrive
ask the question	ask
assembled together	assembled
brief in duration	brief
completely opposite	opposite
continue to remain	remain
consensus of opinion	agreement, consensus
cooperate together	cooperate
desirable benefits	benefits
each and every	each, every
equally as good	as good
few in number	few
filled to capacity	filled
final completion	completion
heat up	heat
join together	join
mix together	mix
mutual cooperation	cooperation
one particular example	an example
past experience (history)	experience
plan ahead	plan
postponed until later	postponed
qualified expert	expert
recur again	recur
seems apparent	seems
still continue	continue
2 P.M. in the afternoon	2 P.M.
unsolved problem	problem
very	(not necessary)
yellow in color	yellow

CORRECTING REDUNDANT WORDING

Identify the redundant phrase and then correct it.

1. I know from past experience that if you plan ahead you can avoid making the same mistakes again.

   _____

   _____

2. Since the committee ran out of time, they had to postpone the discussion of unsolved problems until later.

   _____

   _____

3. It seems apparent that it is very unlikely that we can reach a consensus of opinion on this issue.

   _____

   _____

4. The mechanic joined the pipes together by mixing together epoxy and a filler compound.

   _____

   _____

5. If each and every one of us cooperate together perhaps we can finally complete this task.

   _____

   _____

Commonly Misused Words

DEFINING COMMONLY MISUSED WORDS

English can be a confusing language. Many words, called homonyms, sound alike but have very different meanings. Listed below are some commonly misused words and how to use them.

whether/weather	"Whether" is conditional; "weather" has to do with climate.
there/their/they're	"there is . . ." (or over there); "their" is the possessive of they; "they're" is the contraction for "they are."
it's/its	"It's" is a contraction for "it is"; "its" is possessive of it.
assure/insure/ensure	"Assure" is to convince; "insure" to contract for payment in case of a loss; "ensure" is to make certain or to guarantee.
insight/incite	"insight" is an understanding; "incite" is to arouse.

you're/your	"You're" is the contraction of "you are"; "your" is the possessive of "you."
affect/effect	"affect" (v) means to influence; "effect" (n) means the result of an action.
amount/number	"Amount" applies to mass or bulk; "number" applies to separate units.
continual/continuous	"Continual" means continuing frequently, or in a steady fashion; "continuous" means uninterrupted, unbroken.
farther/further	"Farther" refers to physical distance; "further" means remoteness in time, quantity, or degree.
fewer/less	"Fewer" has to do with numbers of units or individuals (fewer coins); "less" has to do with quantities or amounts of mass or bulk (less money).
over/more than	"Over" should not be used when one means "more than" in referring to numbers.
percent/percentage	"Percent" is written as one word and is used with an exact number. "Percentage" alone never follows a number.

CORRECTING MISUSED WORDS

Circle the correct word in the sentences below:

1. The marketing survey was administered to (over/more than) 10,000 people who live in Syracuse, New York.
2. About 15 (percent/percentage) of the people surveyed preferred Gloss Window Cleaner to Sparkle and Shine.
3. Alice did not care (weather/whether) she attended the soccer game.
4. The purpose of the procedure was to (assure, ensure, insure) that workers would complete the valve alignment correctly.
5. A hurricane in the Gulf of Mexico will (effect/affect) the (weather/whether) in the midwestern states.
6. The dog lost (its/it's) bone.
7. (There, Their, They're) are many reasons that property owners would want to (assure, ensure, insure) their residences.
8. A Zen master has great (insight/incite) into human nature.
9. The package states that this dessert contains (fewer/less) than 70 calories per serving.
10. Is this (you're/your) umbrella?

Errors in Logic/Misplaced Modifiers

DEFINING ERRORS IN LOGIC AND MISPLACED MODIFIERS

Errors in logic occur when the writer does not make the meaning clear. Read this example and decide what the reader meant to say:

I see a lot of kids who eat with bad table manners and it is not a very pleasant sight. This is also helpful when going to a dinner party or on a date.

As you can see, there is no link between kids with bad table manners and going to a dinner party or date. Also, what "this" refers to is not clear.

Misplacing a modifier can also cause problems in logic as in this example:

Walking down the street, a large tree was seen.

Here the modifier "walking down the street" appears to modify "tree." Since trees do not walk down the street, this sentence seems humorous. Many times, the use of passive voice, which we discussed earlier in this section, can create ambiguous references. The sentence can be rewritten as follows:

As I was walking down the street, I saw a large tree.

CORRECTING ERRORS IN LOGIC AND MISPLACED MODIFIERS

To correct misplaced modifiers or illogical sentences, read each sentence carefully and decide what the sentence means, who did the action, and how it can be stated concisely.

Example:

The stolen money was seen by the policeman chasing the thief.

1. Meaning: The policeman was chasing the thief and saw the stolen money.
2. The action: The policeman saw the money.
3. Misplaced modifier: "chasing the thief." (It appears that the money was chasing the thief.)

Corrections:

The policeman saw the stolen money as he chased the thief.

As he chased the thief, the policeman spotted the stolen money.

The policeman chased the thief and saw the stolen money.

Each of the corrections states the main idea of the original idea clearly and concisely.

End Punctuation

DEFINING END PUNCTUATION

End punctuation is punctuation which is placed at the end of a sentence to signify that the thought is complete. There are three types of end punctuation:

1. The period (.) is used at the end of a sentence stating a fact or at the end of a sentence giving a command.

   Example:

   > Bring me the paper which is on the table. (command)
   >
   > George Lawler is my best friend. (statement of fact)

2. The exclamation point (!) is used at the end of a sentence which expresses strong feeling.

   Example:

   > Get out of here or else!
   >
   > Help! The grease in the pan is on fire!

3. The question mark (?) is used at the end of a sentence which asks a question.

   Example:

   > What happened to my candy bar?
   >
   > How much does the prime rib dinner cost?

END-PUNCTUATION EXERCISE

Add appropriate end punctuation to these sentences.

1. Where did you put the book on nuclear physics
2. Take good care of my dog while I'm gone
3. Why did she say that she couldn't work this Friday
4. It's easier to spend money than it is to make it
5. Watch out You could get hurt if you don't watch what you're doing

Comma Usage

COMMA USAGE RULES

Comma use is a very complex concept. This section is just an outline of comma-use rules. Your instructor will cover comma use with you in more

detail and will refer you to additional exercises. However, the following are general rules for comma use.
Use commas when:

☐ The *voice* pauses. This is covered by the other rules.

   Example:

   When you get home (pause), please wash the dog (pause), clean the house (pause), and iron the clothes.

☐ After dates and places

   Example:

   On May 26, 1990, Honeoye, N.Y., will be 200 years old.

☐ With words, phrases, or sentences in a series.

   Example:

   Eat, drink, and be merry for tomorrow we die.

☐ When the information is *NOT* necessary to the meaning of the sentence.

   Example:

   Aimee Cummings, my best friend, is the mayor of Fairport.

☐ With introductory phrases or interjections.

   Example:

   If you send me the report, I'll edit it promptly.

☐ When *two sentences* are joined by "and," "but," "or," "for," or "nor."

   Example:

   He makes mistakes often, but he still keeps his job.

   I wonder how he can make so many mistakes but still keep his job.

COMMA EXERCISE

Read each sentence and insert a comma if necessary.

1. Although we finished the assignment the report will not be processed until Monday.
2. Harley Broom Maintenance Supervisor has worked for Corning Woodworks for twenty years.
3. This computer processes information rapidly but requires a great deal of maintenance.
4. I still have four days of vacation left but I intend to carry them over until next year.
5. The report will not be processed until next Monday although we finished the assignment last week.
6. Contact the supplier order additional parts and arrange for delivery before the end of the week.
7. To be an effective writer you must analyze your audience organize your material and edit your writing ruthlessly.
8. Send me the report when you finish.

9. When you finish send me the report.
10. Buffalo New York is the second most overcast city in America.
11. Red blue and yellow are primary colors.
12. Finish your work check your answers and hand in your paper.
13. Since I didn't file my income tax on April 15 I'm really worried.
14. When you learn to use the comma you will be a more effective writer.
15. When the campaign was over there was no money left in the campaign fund.
16. Because she finished the test early she had time to check her answers.
17. He tried to stay up to watch the movie on television although he was very tired.
18. Oh boy here comes the train!
19. Stevie Wonder a famous American songwriter has had many hit songs.
20. The desk the worktable and the bookcase belong in the library.
21. She tried on eight pairs of shoes but did not purchase any of them.
22. I would like to visit the ocean the state parks and the amusement park.
23. We love to run barefoot over the cool wet sand.
24. In spite of the bad weather predictions the fog lifted the sun shone and the clouds disappeared.
25. The dark dingy musty attic seemed spooky.

The Colon (:) and the Semicolon (;)

USING THE COLON (:)

The primary use of the colon is to introduce a list or series when such expressions as "the following" are used.

Example:

Bring the following with you Monday: a hammer, nails, and a ruler.

The colon is also to be used when a concluding word, phrase, or clause sums up what has been stated before.

Example:

I know one thing for sure about garage sales: the good stuff goes first.

The colon is also used to separate the hour and minute in expressions of time.

Example:

8:13 A.M.

USING THE SEMICOLON (;)

The semicolon is used instead of a coordinating conjunction to separate two independent clauses (and, but, or, for, nor). This use is illustrated in more detail in the section on *run-on sentences*.

Example:

> He came to the party, *and* she left.
> He came to the party; she left.

The semicolon is also used to separate items in a series which contains internal commas. This helps avoid confusion about which words modify which.

Example:

> He brought nice, juicy bananas; crunchy, bright apples; lightly toasted whole wheat bread.

COLON AND SEMICOLON EXERCISE

Add colons and semicolons to the following sentences when needed.

1. The robbery was committed about 832 P.M.
2. Here is your assignment for the week write a process essay.
3. The lake was choppy the moon ricocheted across its surface.
4. The house was located in Brighton an expensive neighborhood.
5. It may not be a fancy house, but I know that it's mine.
6. This task requires the following skills tact and communication skills.
7. Love is one thing marriage is another.
8. While I was leaving, I saw George and Tom.
9. Rose and Gene live in Briar a small town north of Fort Worth, Texas.
10. The following offers were presented one for $5,100, one for $10,200, and one for $3,290.

The Apostrophe (')

The apostrophe is used to show ownership or possession or to take the place of missing letters in a contraction.

Using the Apostrophe to Indicate Possession

Possession is shown by adding an *'s* to singular nouns:

Noun	Possessive	Sentence
girl	girl's	The girl's coat is on the floor.
nickel	nickel's	I bought a nickel's worth of candy.
yesterday	yesterday's	Yesterday's newspaper is on the table.

Plural possessives are formed by adding an apostrophe after the *s*:

Noun	Possessive	Sentence
girls	girls'	The girls' laughter could be heard from the kitchen.

However, if the plural does not end in *s*, then add *'s:*

Noun	Possessive	Sentence
children	children's	Is this the children's department?
men	men's	He went to the men's room.

Using the Apostrophe in Contractions

Another major use of the apostrophe is to take the place of missing letters in contractions.

Examples:

cannot	can't
I have heard	I've heard
He must have gone	He must've gone
It is	it's

APOSTROPHE EXERCISE

Add the apostrophes when necessary.

1. My friend Tommys house is across the street.
2. Tomorrows assignment is really difficult!
3. This paycheck is small for a weeks wages.
4. With the moons light, we were able to find our way.
5. Which magazines do you read?
6. Its about time for class to begin.
7. Whats he doing on Saturday night?
8. I mustve lost my notebook because its not with my books.
9. Saturdays my favorite day of the week.
10. Cant you finish this project before Mondays conference?

Using Transitional Words

Transitional words are words which are used to link ideas and create a flow between sentences. They can be used to emphasize comparisons, illustrate cause and effect relationships, or establish a sequence. However, they should be used sparingly or they will lose their effectiveness.

Some commonly used transitional words are listed in the table below.

Comparison	On one hand, on the other hand, likewise, in this instance, similarly, both, also, in addition
Contrast	However, conversely, on the other hand, in contrast, yet, although
Previous reference	As mentioned, previously, then, as stated before, considering that
Cause and effect	Consequently, if . . . then, as a result, because, since, therefore, as an effect, for that reason
Sequence or time	Now, before, concurrently, afterwards, earlier, in the past, previously, prior to, subsequently, simultaneously, then, therefore, until now, formerly, later, meanwhile, repeatedly, first, second, third
Closing	In conclusion, finally, in summary, to sum up, to conclude

Compare these two paragraphs and decide which is more effective.

> Potting a plant requires skill and attention to detail. Select a large pot. Fill the bottom of the pot with small stones. Fill about half of the pot with potting soil. Prepare the plant by removing dead leaves. Then prune back upper growth approximately one-third. Trim off any broken roots. Place the plant in the pot. Fill the pot firmly with potting soil. Tamp the soil down firmly. Water the plant thoroughly.

> Potting a plant requires skill and attention to detail. After selecting a large pot, fill the bottom with small stones and *then* add about a half pot of potting soil. *Next,* prepare the plant by removing dead leaves and broken roots and by pruning upper growth back approximately one-third. *Finally,* place the plant in the pot and fill the pot firmly with potting soil. After tamping down the soil firmly, water the plant thoroughly.

By combining ideas and using transitional words, the writer can create much more cohesive and interesting writing.

USING TRANSITIONAL WORDS

Revise the paragraph below by combining ideas and using transitional words.

> Camping provides inexpensive entertainment for the family. By camping, a family can save money on meals. Instead of eating in restaurants, a family can have the adventure of cooking dinner over a campfire.

Camping fees are very low. State Parks charge an average of $7 per night. This is much less than motels. Rather than going to movies and theme parks, families can enjoy walks in the woods and swimming for free. The self-reliance of camping creates memories for all. These are worth more than gold.

The Half-Sentence Transition

In addition to using transitional words to connect ideas, a writer can use the half-sentence transition. In the "half-sentence transition," the writer restates the essence of a previous paragraph in the first half of a sentence that introduces the next paragraph. In the second half of the sentence the writer introduces the next idea to be developed.

Notice how the essay on the following page effectively uses this device. It was written by an American teacher working and studying in Japan. Read the essay through once. Then reread it and locate the half-sentences. You will note that these sentences summarize or paraphrase what was previously said and integrate that information with the next idea.

MY WALLET

My old leather wallet was a gift from my mother. When it was new, it was a lovely shade of rose, but years of hard use have left it a greyish pink color. Nevertheless, old and cracked as it is, my wallet still faithfully serves to hold many of the items I need every day.

A place to keep money is, of course, the primary function of a wallet, and mine has special sections for coins, paper bills, my dollar checkbook, and even a place for my two yen cash cards. Over the years, thousands of dollars and millions of yen have gone in—and out—of my wallet, but I can find only a few old receipts in a language I cannot read folded in among the paper yen notes to prove this fact.

While money comes and goes from my wallet, it also contains several things which I never remove: two driver's licenses, one for Japan and one for the U.S., the alien registration card which allows me to stay in Japan, and identification cards for Temple University and the American Club. In this complicated modern world, without these little cards, I would have no identity, and no right to claim a place in society.

Along with money and identification cards, my wallet also holds an odd collection of other items which defy categorization: calling cards, two U.S. stamps, notes from my husband and children, Tokyo phone numbers on bits of paper, a five cruziero bill from São Paulo days, and old grocery lists. These things must have been important to me at one time, otherwise they would not have been put in my wallet, but now I can only wonder why I carry them around with me every day, everywhere I go. Perhaps, just as the identification cards are a public declaration of who I am, this half-forgotten minutiae of daily living serves in a personal way to remind me of the identities I have: as wife—mother—teacher—student—American—resident—in—Japan. Perhaps the primary purpose of a wallet is to hold money, but it may be that money is the least important of the items we find there.

Editing

DEFINING EDITING

Editing is the art of analyzing your writing to improve the structure and sharpen the focus of your writing. It also includes recognizing and correcting errors in mechanics and punctuation.

EDITING EXERCISES

The following paragraphs are provided for editing practice. Analyze each to determine the main and supporting ideas. Then decide what material can be deleted or combined to create more concise writing. When you have finished, ask your instructor to check your work.

EDITING EXERCISE 1

This paragraph contains run-on sentences, fragments, agreement errors, and wordiness.

Every person should be married. Because their life is not complete without the one-to-one companionship that marriage causes. You know, life is lonely, it is hard to work all day and then come home to a house which is empty. I feel that the best part of the day is when I come home and find my loved one waiting for me, it makes the whole day after all. After all, it's a jungle out there. At home at least I'm safe. Love conquers all, even a bad case of college student blues.

EDITING EXERCISE 2

This paragraph contains punctuation, capitalization, agreement, and sentence-structure errors. Read it carefully for typographical errors and for wordiness.

There are many reasons why you should come to university of florida. One reason is that it haves many internationally nown fields of study. Another reason that you should no is the reason that faculty members seems to care about the students, most of the time students can get tutoring or extra help from faculty members after class or in the lab. Besides that students can also get financial aid. Including scholarships and student loans. Final, U of f offers a professional climate of learning which help each students to succeed in their field. An important consideration for the future.

EDITING EXERCISE 3

This writing contains examples of sentence fragments, run-on sentences, and wordiness.

Although many of us think about retirement, few of us really make the best use of our retirement funds. It is important to keep in mind that one of the best investments for the future is the IRA, a tax-deferred annuity which is available upon retirement. This is an excellent savings plan for the working person, it encourages the systematic setting aside of funds and provides a needed tax deduction during high earning years. The IRA will not take the place of other retirement plans, but it will provide an excellent supplement for one's retirement years.

EDITING EXERCISE 4

This paragraph contains choppy sentences which can be corrected through editing and sentence combining.

A nuclear reactor works as result of fission. Fission is the splitting of atoms. The atoms are bombarded by neutrons. When a neutron splits an atom, more neutrons are formed. Two new elements are also formed. The released neutrons split into other atoms. This causes more reactions. In the reactor core, fission is controlled. This is done by the insertion of cadmium rods. Cadmium is used because of its ability to absorb neutrons. When an atom is split, neutrons are released. Energy in the form of heat is produced. Water surrounding the reactor core is heated. It vaporizes into steam. The steam leaves the reactor to drive the turbine. The turbine generates electricity. The steam is then condensed either in a cooling tower or by fresh water. After the steam is condensed into water, it is pumped back into the reactor. This is how a nuclear plant works.

EDITING EXERCISE 5

This paragraph contains several run-on sentences and comma errors.

Good writing requires careful planning and organization. The first step is to think up a topic which you like, are knowledgeable about, and can research if necessary, then you have to limit your topic. This is important if you don't limit your topic you may end up writing more than you want to. Next you must develop a thesis statement, this is a one sentence statement of what your paper is about. After you have the thesis statement develop ideas which related directly to it. Now that you have the main ideas think of examples details or reasons to support them. It is important to be specific. When you have arranged your material carefully begin to write your essay. When you have finished proofread it, this will help you get rid of errors in sentence structure spelling and punctuation.

Proofreading

DEFINING PROOFREADING

Proofreading is a technique used to identify errors, usually typographical or mechanical, in your writing. This is the final check after you have completed your essay.

PROOFREADING TIPS

Here are some tips to help you proofread your writing:

1. Set your writing aside for a few minutes. This will allow you to see your work from a new perspective.
2. Limit your field of vision. You can do this by using two clean envelopes to isolate each line or sentence as you read it individually.
3. Read each line of your writing from *bottom to top* to locate mechanical errors. This will help you find typographical errors, mechanical errors, and spelling errors.
4. Read each sentence individually for sentence structure and logic errors. Make certain sentences are concise and complete.
5. Read the entire writing through from beginning to end for coherence and content.
6. If appropriate, ask a fellow student or instructor to look over your work for errors.
7. Read your essay aloud.

PROOFREADING EXERCISE

Using the techniques we have discussed, mark the errors in the following paragraph. Then correct the errors and have the instructor check your work.

Rochester Institute of Technology (R.I.T.) is known world-wide as the premiere collage in tehnologic areas. Amoung it's most well-known areas is cumpoter technalogy and printing. Last year a lone RIT spend 4.2 millyon dollars on computers. Alot of faculty and allmost all RIT students will be computer literature by 1989. Which is a major new innovation in the educational busniness. The college of Printing offer many coarses whitch are attended by students from a round the world. Coming from as far as China. These lucky graduates find job easy in an otherwise hard market this goes to show that rit is by far the most best university in technology.

WRITING YOUR WAY EVALUATION FORM

NAME _____

DATE _____   ESSAY _____

COMMENTS/ASSIGNMENTS

Content	
Organization Attention–Getter Purpose Topic Sentence Introduction Background Information Supporting Information Transitions Conclusion	
Sentence Structure Fragments Run–Ons Choppy Sentences Wordy Sentences Misplaced Modifiers Subject/Verb Agreement Other	
Verbs Verb Forms Verb Tense Infinitives Passive/Active Voice Other	
Language Dictionary Thesaurus Spelling Word Forms Redundant Wording Nonspecific Language Misused Words Articles Pronoun Use Other	
Punctuation Comma Apostrophe Colon/Semicolon Other _____	
Editing	
Proofreading	

Note: When your instructor returns this form, enter the information on the Evaluation Summary Form at the back of your book. This will help you keep track of your writing progress.

WRITING YOUR WAY EVALUATION SUMMARY FORM

ASSIGNMENTS

Content

Organization
Attention-Getter

Purpose

Topic Sentence

Introduction

Background Information

Supporting Information

Transitions

Conclusion

Sentence Structure
Fragments

Run-Ons

Choppy Sentences

Wordy Sentences

Misplaced Modifiers

Subject/Verb Agreement

Other

Verbs
Verb Forms

Verb Tense

Infinitives

Passive/Active Voice

Other

Language
Dictionary

Thesaurus

Spelling

Word Forms

Redundant Wording

Nonspecific Language

Misused Words

Articles

Pronoun Use

Other

Punctuation
Comma

Apostrophe

Colon/Semicolon

Other _____

Editing

Proofreading

Note: When your teacher returns the Evaluation Form, enter the information on this page. This will help you keep track of the areas you have improved in and those that need work.

Index